Dale Coulter has done  an important and timely work that addresses an issue vital to the life of individual believers, the congregations in which they worship, and the entire body of Christ. This volume does not provide an easy treatment of the sensitive issue of holiness. Rather, it is a thorough consideration of the subject, providing a solid Biblical and theological base for informing our understanding and teaching on the topic. Coulter's work will go a long way in helping pastors and teachers recover and clearly communicate the theme of holiness from the perspective of Israel's covenant relationship with God, its outworking in the New Testament community, and its implications for the contemporary church.

Reverend Estrelda Alexander, Ph.D.
Associate Professor of Theology
Regent University

For all of us who have experienced forgiveness in Christ and yet struggle with sin or old habits, this book provides a clear explanation of a way out. Like a physician diagnosing an illness, Dr. Coulter examines the disease of sin and focuses our attention on the "double cure." In the past, much writing about holiness was stymied in negative, stingy tones of "ought" or "should" or "don't." By focusing on the beauty of God, Coulter opens our minds to the majesty of God's character and reminds us that God gives "beauty for ashes."

Terry L. Cross, Ph.D.
Dean, School of Religion
Professor of Theology
Lee University

Dale Coulter's call to revisit the meaning of holiness is a timely message for today's church. It is a positive appeal that presents holiness as the joyful outcome of a restored relationship with God. For Coulter, holiness is not a dreary existence. It is a life of wonder and joyful fellowship with the triune God, who heals us of our brokenness and transforms us into the image of Christ.

Cheryl Bridges Johns
Professor of Discipleship and Christian
  Formation
Church of God Theological Seminary

God's great and beautiful promise is that those who trust fully in Christ will share fully in His life; we will be holy as He is holy. The call to holiness is the most neglected and misunderstood of the central teachings of the Scriptures, even among those who were born into the Holiness Movement. This timeless message has never been needed more. Dr. Coulter has provided us with that rare gift of a readable, scholarly book on a topic essential to the Christian journey. He writes with the passion of a prophet, the clarity of a sage, and the pulse of a poet. This book should be read, circulated and studied by all who desire God.

Jackie David Johns, Ph.D.
Director of the Doctor of Ministry Program
Professor of Discipleship
Church of God Theological Seminary
Pastor, New Covenant Church of God

HOLINESS

HOLINESS
The Beauty of Perfection

Dale M. Coulter

Pathway
PRESS

Book Editor: Wanda Griffith
Editorial Assistant: Tammy Hatfield
Copy Editors: Elizabeth Hightower
Esther Metaxas

Library of Congress Catalog Card Number: 2004093694
ISBN: 0-87148-068-9
Copyright © 2004 by Pathway Press
Cleveland, Tennessee 37311
All Rights Reserved
Printed in the United States of America

To Esther, Bella and Sophie

Contents

Foreword

I have known Dale Coulter for many years. In fact, we entered a ministry partnership over 10 years ago when he became part of the pastoral staff at the church where I served as senior pastor in Orlando, Florida. That ministry partnership has evolved into a close personal friendship.

Even from those early days of ministry, it was apparent that Dale had a passion for learning and communicating Biblical truth in a way that was culturally relevant and theologically sound. That passion has determined the priorities of his life. Over the years, I have often said to him, "When you write your first book . . ." I knew the day would come when the convictions in his head and his heart would find expression through his hands in the form of the written word.

In this book, he deals with a subject that is often misunderstood and somewhat neglected, even in Evangelical circles. With clarity, understanding and insight, he presents the subject of holiness from a perspective that motivates rather than intimidates the reader. An understanding of holiness is essential to our relationship with God and foundational to our call as Christians to make disciples. Throughout the book,

Dale uses terms and illustrations that help the reader grasp the truth concerning holiness.

As I read each chapter, I found myself saying, "Yes," which, in this context, is the equivalent to "Amen." When I came to the final page of the last chapter, I found myself exclaiming aloud, "Praise the Lord," as I considered the blessings of a holy life. This book will help you see holiness as more than a theological concept—you will begin to view it as a transforming truth that influences every part of your life. Whether you are a pastor or a layperson, this book will encourage, enlighten and enrich your life. I recommend it as an excellent resource for a balanced and Biblical view of holiness.

Shalom!

—Mitchell E. Corder
Administrative Bishop of the Church of God in Kansas

Preface

During the summer of 2000, my Aunt Lois came to visit my family at our home in Cleveland, Tennessee. Little did I know at the time that this first visit would also be her last. She made the long trip from Florida with my parents because she wanted to see our new house and take a break from the daily demands she faced. During the visit, we decided to take a trip to Fields of the Wood—a small park near Murphy, North Carolina. This park, which the Church of God of Prophecy operates, has several monuments dedicated to various Biblical and Pentecostal themes.

When you visit places that are part of your history, as this place was for my family, they conjure images of your own personal journey. At least, this was the case for us that day. As we walked around the park, we talked about the Church of God and its emphasis on holiness and ways that emphasis had shaped us.

On the way back to Cleveland, my aunt began to talk about her own experience of holiness. "I believe in holiness," she said, as we drove around the winding roads back down the mountain. "Dale," she continued, "I remember going down to the front of the church and experiencing the power of sanctification at work in my life. I felt the presence of the Holy Spirit, beginning at the top of my head and running to the bottom of my feet. I left the altar and I knew I was clean before God."

Her words left a mark on me, but even more impressive was her hunger for holiness. As she spoke, I could sense her passionate commitment to pursue God at all costs. She exemplified a quest for the beauty of holiness our forefathers had.

In this book, I have tried to recapture some of that passion for the holy life my aunt possessed. This passion is what caused men and women of the past to rush to the altar, prostrate themselves before God and pray, beseeching Him to fill them with His presence. They had caught a vision of something better than what they already had. What was it that attracted them to holiness? It was a glimpse of the beauty of God's perfection. Like a bride beholds her bridegroom with transfixed eyes, they beheld the beauty of the Lord and ran passionately toward Him.

Make no mistake, this is a theological book. If we want to rekindle a passion for holiness, we need to engage in the strenuous task of doing "good theology." Contrary to what some people may think, good theology gives rise to spiritual health and wholeness. Like plowing a field, the work may be difficult, but the crops are worth the effort. Doing the hard work of developing good theology will produce a lifetime of good crops. Bad theology has the opposite effect and can do serious damage to people. Consequently, I have tried to offer help in developing a good holiness theology.

Acknowledgments

There are many people who deserve my thanks. I appreciate my students at Lee University who always ask insightful questions and push me to clarify my points. They have proven to be stimulating partners in my attempt to develop my ideas about holiness. In particular, my student worker, Amy Coffin, has been helpful in making photocopies, tracking down sources and making numerous trips to Squires Library.

I am also grateful for the conversations with Drs. Todd Hibbard and Brad Frazier, my colleagues and friends. They kept me from making too many mistakes.

I would also like to express appreciation to my church family, the New Covenant Church of God. When Esther and I came to Cleveland, we were looking for a place to call home, and New Covenant became that place.

Several people generously read parts of the manuscript as I was preparing it. My thanks go to Drs. Jackie and Cheryl Bridges Johns, my pastors at New Covenant, who read many of the chapters. I am also grateful to my colleagues, Drs. Terry Cross and Todd Hibbard, who also read chapters and gave me feedback.

Thanks to the members of the covenant group I lead—Matthew Covert, Tracy and Joylita Terpstra, Sam and Erin Burleson, Vernice Blackaby, Kindra Green and

Ashley Pollak—who allowed me to use some of my chapters as discussion material during our meetings.

In addition, I would like to thank Dr. Bill George, editor in chief at Pathway Press, who read some of the initial drafts and encouraged me to complete the project.

All of these readers helped shape the material through their encouragement and comments, which I trust has made this a better book.

My thanks also go to Administrative Bishop Mitchell Corder and Wendy, Sarah and Hannah for their friendship over the years.

Finally, this book is dedicated to my wife, Esther, and our daughters, Bella and Sophie, for the beauty and joy that they bring into my life.

A song Esther wrote expresses well my own prayer:

Show me Your beauty in the rightness of Your ways,
Show me Your beauty in the sameness of my days,
Show me Your beauty in the wonder of Your face,
Then I will say that I am satisfied.

PART I

THE PURPOSE
OF HOLINESS

CHAPTER 1

Why Forgiveness Is Not Enough

May the God of peace himself sanctify you entirely; and may your spirit and soul and body be kept sound and blameless at the coming of our Lord Jesus Christ. The one who calls you is faithful, and he will do this (1 Thessalonians 5:23, 24).

I forgive you," she said.

"You do?" Jim could feel his tense muscles slowly relax. All that mattered was hearing her say those words. This infidelity was the latest episode in a long battle to control his urges, and he needed to know everything was all right.

"I have forgiven you before and I'll do it again," Heather added. "The problem is not my forgiveness."

"I don't know what you mean."

"Don't you? Jim, as long as you continue to behave this way, things will not get better. Unless you change, all the forgiveness in the world will not be enough to save our marriage."

It may seem odd to begin this book with a chapter that seems to run counter to one of the basic tenets of

the Christian message. After all, Scripture clearly empha-
sizes that forgiveness of sins is part of our faith (Acts
13:38; Ephesians 1:7). In fact, the promise of forgiveness lies at the heart of the gospel message. God forgives sinners not because they deserve it, but because
of His gracious and merciful kindness extended
through Jesus Christ.

As important as forgiveness is, it only deals with
part of the problem. God not only must forgive us of
the wrongs we have done, He also must heal us of the
damage those sinful actions inflict upon us so that we
do not commit them again. When we begin to see how
God heals us, we take our first steps toward understanding why He calls us to holy living.

To explain why God's work extends beyond forgiveness, we should begin with an exploration of
human sinfulness. It may be helpful to think of sin as
both a disease and as guilt. When we think of sin as
guilt, we are considering it as a criminal act in viola-
tion of God's laws. This is how many people think of
sin when they offer definitions such as "missing the
mark" or "disobeying God." Just as criminals incur
guilt and punishment as a result of their crimes, sinners incur guilt and punishment as a result of their
sins. Guilt must be forgiven.

Conversely, when we think of sin as a disease, we
are considering it as a defect inherited from Adam and
Eve and the internal damage inflicted upon us by our
sinful actions and the sinful actions of others. In the
same way a disease weakens the body and strips it of

life, sin weakens us and leads to our spiritual demise. Whereas guilt must be forgiven, a disease must be cured. Sin functions as a disease in three ways: as a self-inflicted disease, as a social disease and as an inborn disease. Once we explore these three aspects of sin, the nature and purpose of forgiveness will become clearer.

SIN AS A SELF-INFLICTED DISEASE

Paul's explanation of sinfulness in Romans is a good place to start an examination of sin as a self-inflicted disease. Following the prologue (1:1-17), the opening chapters attempt to persuade the reader that both Jews and Gentiles stand in the same position before God. A central thread running throughout this section is the relationship between human choices and sinful consequences. Paul describes the descent into sin as a series of choices that leads an individual into increasing degrees of corruption. This is the self-inflicted disease of sin in which each sinful choice warps a person's pattern of thought and behavior. The end result is that the person brings about his or her own destruction.

The downward slide has its origins in what Biblical scholar James Dunn describes as "misdirected religion."[1] That is, it begins with a failure to recognize God as God (vv. 18-23). The apostle Paul also defines this failure as a suppression of the truth. It would be overly simplistic to think that what Paul means here is that these persons did not practice the correct religious rituals. The fact that Paul applies the same critique to his fellow Jews in chapter 2 should be enough to counter such an interpretation. Paul was not talking about individuals who failed to attend church every time the doors opened or who failed to say the correct prayers. Instead, they failed to recognize God and thereby failed to shape their lives in light of God's purposes.

As one commentator suggests, "to acknowledge God as my Creator means to recognize that God has a claim on me that no creature can make, indeed, the ultimate and immediate claim on my very existence."[2] This is the truth that is being suppressed by Jews and Gentiles. Jews, who have the law of Moses, and Gentiles, who have a law written on their consciences, both fail to shape their lives in light of the divine purpose communicated through these laws (2:12-16).[3] The failure to recognize the Creator is a failure to know the direction one's life should take. Only the divine Creator fully understands the purpose for His creation.

For Paul, the problem of not living in light of God's purposes reveals itself in individuals who choose their own ways. He states that they "claimed to be wise" (1:22, *NIV*) about the direction for their lives because they thought they knew the truth. After making their choices, however, they had inflicted so much damage upon themselves that they could no longer recognize the truth: "they exchanged the truth of God for a lie" (v. 25, *NIV*). This inability to recognize the truth does not simply refer to truth about God, but also about themselves, their relationships to their fellow humans and their relationships to the entire created order.

What kind of damage does Paul envision? He seems

to be suggesting that a kind of self-inflicted blindness ensues from the corruption produced by personal choices. As he declares in verse 28, "Since they did not see fit to acknowledge God, God gave them up to a debased mind and to things that should not be done." The self-inflicted damage of sin brings such disorder that the individual is no longer capable of relating to God, himself, others or even creation in the appropriate ways.

The example of adultery illustrates how sinful choices damage an individual. When a husband commits adultery, he incurs guilt for that sin, but he also inflicts damage on his soul. He can ask forgiveness from God and his wife and receive it, but that forgiveness cannot completely repair the damage caused by his action. Consider all of the thoughts and actions leading up to an act of adultery. A married person does not wake up one day and simply decide, "I'm going to commit adultery." Rather, his act of adultery comes at the end of a series of choices: repeatedly entertaining sexual thoughts, convincing himself that his wife does not satisfy him, devaluing his wife to convince himself that his action is justified, and so on.

All of those choices inflict damage by creating sinful patterns of thought and behavior, clouding his mind with lies about himself, his needs and his wife. This corruption eventually gives birth to the act of adultery. The deceptive nature of these patterns is that they usually begin while the husband and wife are struggling through real marital issues. However, in the case of adultery, the spouse's response to those issues places him on a path that will damage not just himself, but also his wife, his marriage and his children. This may be what James means by, "Each one is tempted when he is drawn away by his own desires and enticed. Then, when desire has conceived, it gives birth to sin; and sin, when it is full-grown, brings forth death" (1:14, 15, *NKJV*).

Although repentance and forgiveness are necessary first steps in recovery, the damage cannot be repaired by simply asking for forgiveness. There is a history of choices giving rise to the act of adultery that must be overcome. The evil fruit born from these choices darkens the mind so that the individual believes a lie. In our example, there are multiple lies the husband believes about himself, his own needs, his wife and his marriage. Ultimately, the adulterer chooses to believe the lie that committing the act of adultery is actually good for him and only through an extramarital affair can he have his needs met, or be fulfilled as a human being.

To repair the damage, the person must make good choices to undo his bad choices. To put it in Biblical terms, the adulterer is in bondage to sin because he has developed sinful patterns of thinking and behaving. The sin must be broken by that same person choosing to change by the Spirit's power. Repentance and forgiveness are the first steps down the long path of reversing the damage his choices have created.

Jane's story illustrates my point. Jane was living with a drug dealer in an extravagantly furnished apartment. Did she mind living with a drug dealer? No, because he made a large sum of money every week. At least, that is what Jane said. What about when the drug dealer hit her? This did not seem to matter as much as having nice furniture and a nice place to live. It seems that Jane cared most about having material possessions. As long as she could wear designer clothes, drive an expensive car and live in a luxurious apartment, the occasional beatings and the drugs could be endured.

Doesn't Jane see how damaging that kind of lifestyle is? It seems so clear to us that her relationship with a drug dealer is unhealthy and dangerous, but it's not clear to Jane. In fact, if Jane were here today, she might argue that she had the "good life." It would be too simplistic to say that Jane saw the good life as having material possessions. Instead, she derived pleasure from the overall image created by the designer clothes and lavish lifestyle. According to her, that's the good life, and maintaining the image requires a certain amount of money. Jane is no longer capable of recognizing the truth about her situation. As Romans 1:28 says, "Since they did not see fit to acknowledge God, God gave them up to a debased mind and to things that should not be done." There is a kind of self-inflicted blindness that produces self-destructive behavior.

To clarify what I mean by the blindness that sin produces, consider the difference between perception and reality. The way a person sees an event (his perception) may be different from what actually happened. If I looked at a sunflower and said, "That flower has lovely red petals," my wife would wonder if I were going color-blind. The truth is, sunflowers have yellow petals, not red ones. But my perception was very different.

Everyone has perceptions about life. Jane's perception was that the image created by material possessions led to the "good life." The adulterer may perceive that adultery is good for him. Neither of these perceptions reflects the truth, but our patterns of thinking and behaving shape the way we perceive the world, including what we believe is good for us. As we make sinful choices, we develop sinful patterns. Because our sinful patterns of thinking cause us to interpret or understand events in a particular way, they can keep us from recognizing the truth. We can become so blind to the truth that our perceptions no longer reflect reality. These patterns also cause us to misunderstand ourselves, our relationships to others and our relationships to our world. This self-inflicted blindness gives rise to self-destructive behavior. Paul's response is to claim that only by living in light of God's purpose or truth about ourselves can we find the good life.

SIN AS A SOCIAL DISEASE

Self-inflicted blindness may have been just part of the story for Paul. An early commentary on Romans written by Pelagius reveals another dimension to Romans 1: the social context for sin.[4] Although Pelagius was eventually branded a heretic by the church, we can still learn some things from him.

When Pelagius read Romans 1, he did not see a group of disconnected individuals who made choices apart from one another, but a series of social networks in which groups of people were impacted by one another's choices.

When someone enters the world at birth, he or she becomes part of a family. The family to which that person belongs lives in a neighborhood that forms part of a city. The city is part of a region, like Indianapolis is part of the Midwest, or Boston is part of the Northeast. Finally, the region is part of a country.

We should think about each of these as forming a series of concentric circles with family at the center (see diagram). As sociologists remind us, we learn who we are and how we should behave from the social networks to which we belong.

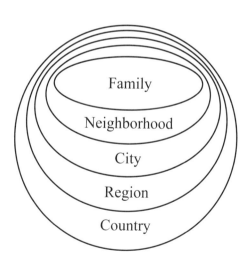

In his commentary, Pelagius reminds us that our choices to sin do not occur in a vacuum. We enter this world as part of a social network, the most immediate example of which is a family. At the center of that family are a mother, father and older siblings whose choices remain intertwined with one another like strands of rope. The choices of the mother and father impact the children, and if their choices are sinful ones, these choices certainly damage their children as well as themselves.

We learn from Pelagius' interpretation of Romans that this self-inflicted blindness gets passed from parent to child in a vicious cycle. This is a kind of socially-inflicted blindness, aggravated by wounds received from others. This kind of sin might be best understood as spiritual pollution because it has to do with the contaminating effects of the choices people make.[5] Every choice we make affects those around us, and if they are sinful, we can be certain that those choices pollute and contaminate.

To return to Jane's story, it seems that her blindness is self-inflicted. But a closer look at Jane's life shows how her parents shaped her perception of the world and what was good for her. There was a decisive moment in Jane's life when she was enjoying a meal with some friends in a fast-food restaurant. While eating, she noticed her father on the other side of the restaurant. Jane went to say hello to her father, only to discover that he did not recognize her. Her father had been on crack cocaine for a number of years, and the result of his choices was that he could not even see his own daughter. That incident burned something into Jane's heart. It robbed her of being a daughter loved by a father, and taught her that she needed to steel up her own heart and become calloused to survive in life. Like dumping toxic waste into a beautiful park, sinful choices defiled Jane and perpetuated themselves in her.

Although I have focused on extreme patterns of thinking and behaving, there are subtle ones as well. For example, how does racism perpetuate itself? Are children born racist, or are they born to racist parents who communicate sinful ideologies to them? In the recent past, there were entire communities that taught their children to hate and mistreat others who were not like them. Entire communities were given over to racism, despite Scriptural passages like Paul's proclamation that in Christ there is no longer Jew or Greek, slave or free, male or female (Galatians 3:28). Unfortunately, racism is alive and well in our present culture. Its continued presence helps us see that the problem of misguided religion has more subtle versions.

The fact that every person is born into a social context and taught what is important and how to behave in that context provides additional insight into the nature of sin as a disease. Sinful patterns of thought or behavior are often passed along from parents to children. Sometimes children simply pick up on what their parents say or do; other times children are wounded by their parents' lack of love or attention and replicate the same behavior to their own children. The same is true of entire communities that embody sinful practices like racism. This does not excuse anyone from sinful behavior, but it paints a realistic picture of how certain kinds of sinful behavior emerge in people.

We must never fail to see how sinful choices pollute and pervert those around us. When we wound others by passing along sinful patterns of thinking and behaving, we contaminate the spiritual environment in which we live. This kind of spiritual pollution has toxic effects on those around us and is one of the ways in which we perpetuate the disease of sin in the lives of others.

SIN AS AN INBORN DISEASE

The social nature of sin and the self-inflicted blindness it creates can lead to several questions. How did humanity get in this state? What prompts people to make such self-destructive choices over the courses of their lives? What causes parents to do damage to their children? What causes those children to inflict the same damage on their children? While I have offered partial answers to these questions, theologians have most often appealed to the idea that people enter the world at birth already infected with the disease of sin.

We can begin to get a sense of what it means to be infected with this disease in Romans 5:12—8:3, where Paul depicts sin as an internal power that rules over people.[6] He describes people as "slaves of sin" because sin has dominion and reigns in their lives (cf. 6:6, 12, 14, 17). As an internal power, sin also brings people into captivity (7:23). It operates as a disease, warping the person's natural tendencies and moving him or her step-by-step toward destruction.

Paul gives clues on how sin exercises its control over people. Sin attaches itself to human desires and leads them astray. It produces sinful cravings that prompt individuals to make destructive choices (6:12). When Paul gives examples of how sin abuses the law of God, he intentionally focuses on coveting (7:7-12). The term used in 6:12 to refer to the lusts of sin and in 7:7-12 to refer to coveting is the same: *epithymia*. While the term generally refers to human desires or passions, in this context Paul used it to describe passions that have gone astray.

At its core, coveting is misdirecting one's passions so that one craves something that belongs to someone else. As Luke Timothy Johnson notes, Paul has in mind the "desiring disease" in which individuals desire inappropriate objects.[7] If we recall that Paul describes God giving people who pursue their own cravings over to those desires (1:24), we can see how the argument has come full circle. As an inborn disease, sin affects our desires, turning them away from their natural courses to unnatural ones.

Theologians have understood Paul's idea of sinful desires to indicate that humans possess a fallen or sinful nature. Paul tends to use the term *flesh* as shorthand for the compulsion we feel when our desires pull us in a sinful direction. In fact, the *NIV* translates the term *flesh* as "sinful nature." The phrase *sinful nature* communicates the idea that all humans are defective in some way. Their wills and desires do not function as they should. Instead of desires pushing them toward God and causing them to make right choices, they experience just the opposite.

Thomas Aquinas, a 13th century theologian, helps us understand what it means to possess a sinful nature.[8] Aquinas suggests that a sinful nature functions like a sickness. When a person is sick, his or her body cannot perform as it should. The sickness is a condition that prevents the body from operating at peak capacity.

Diseases usually cripple the body in some way and prevent people from doing everything they could do if they were in good health. Some diseases are more crippling than others. For example, Alzheimer's is a disease that slowly cripples the brain so that a person loses the ability to think. In its most severe form, Alzheimer's causes a person to lose the ability to speak and function in other basic ways. All of these symptoms result from the disease's attack on brain cells. A sinful nature affects us in much the same way, crippling us so that we cannot function as we should. A sinful nature deprives us of spiritual health. We can get a clearer sense of how this disease affects our desires by separating these desires into two types.

1. *All humans have natural desires*. These desires are fundamental drives—like the drive to eat, the drive to know things, the drive for companionship and the drive for sex. We call these natural desires *needs* because they are actually good for us. For example, anyone who

loses the drive to eat will soon die. Likewise, the drive for sex is necessary for the procreation of children and the intimacy of marriage.

2. *Humans also have acquired desires.*[9] In addition to the drive to eat, some humans have a desire to eat chocolate while others have a desire to eat pizza. We can call the desire to eat chocolate an acquired desire because it is a "want" we acquire on top of our need to eat. The same point could be made about the drive to have sex. Sometimes there are acquired desires to have sex with a particular person. Although the drive for sex itself is not wrong, the acquired desire may be bad if it is directed toward the wrong person. While natural desires help identify our needs, acquired desires point us toward our wants.

The problem of sin is that our acquired desires often work against our natural desires. My desire to consume too much chocolate may work against me because it could lead to weight gain, which can cause health complications. The same can be said for a husband's desire to have sex with anyone other than his wife. The disease of sin manifests itself in this battle between our acquired desires and our natural desires. In other words, sin manifests itself in the way our "wants" work against our "needs."

We are moved by misdirected desires to do or acquire things that do not promote our own well-being. Acquired desires create perceptions about what is good for us. The man who is about to commit adultery has an acquired desire to have a relationship with another woman. If he gives in to the acquired desire, it reinforces his sinful behavior. With enough reinforcement, the desire becomes a habit from which the man cannot escape. In this way, sin becomes an internal power compelling us to do things.

Our sinful nature manifests itself when our acquired desires drive us in directions that are spiritually unhealthy. We come into the world diseased and our natural and acquired desires do not work in harmony to promote our own well-being. We need to eat, but we want to eat chocolate. We need to have shelter and clothing, but we want to own a five-bedroom house and wear designer clothes. We need sex for marital intimacy and the procreation of children, but we want sex for recreational purposes.

All of our uncontrolled passions and lusts lead to murder, strife, adultery and violence. If we could get all of our desires to work together and move in the right direction, then every choice we made would be for God's glory and our good.

Paul does not leave his readers guessing about the destruction produced by sinful desires. "The wages of sin is death" (Romans 6:23). In fact, a glance at chapters 5 and 6 shows how often Paul links sin and death. Death entered the world through sin and reigned from Adam to Moses (6:12, 14, 17). Paul describes sin's reign as one occurring "in death" (5:21), which suggests that the disease of sin produces and thrives in an environment of decay. If the disease of sin is not cured, sinful desires ultimately bring death.

As a disease, sin infects humanity in many ways. It is a self-inflicted disease because through choices we warp our patterns of behaving and thinking so that they become self-destructive. But this is not the whole story. Sin is also a highly infectious disease that pollutes our environment. The sinful actions of others contaminate us and can reproduce themselves in our lives. In the end, it is best to see this disease as in us from the beginning. It is the desiring disease in which our desires work against one another and lead us down the wrong paths. Unless God cures us, we cannot escape the inevitable culmination of this disease in our own spiritual deaths.

FORGIVENESS AND SALVATION

Throughout this opening chapter, I have intentionally avoided the topic of forgiveness. We need to realize that forgiveness is not enough to cure the disease of sin. Many Christians just want to know they are forgiven and don't sense the need to be transformed and healed. They are content with a minimalist approach to Christianity, asking, "What is the least I have to do?" For them, forgiveness becomes the sum total of salvation.

Forgiveness does have a role to play. In fact, it is a crucial aspect of our salvation. We could call forgiveness the gate of salvation, because it is God's invitation to enter His restoration program. Although forgiveness deals with the guilt we have for sinful deeds and thoughts, it does not cure the disease of sin. When we fail to grasp this larger purpose of salvation, forgiveness becomes a form of cheap grace.

We can see how forgiveness opens the path to complete fellowship with God by briefly taking note of what people are guilty of when they sin. The guilt for sinful actions or thoughts does not reside in missing just any mark. Nor should it be thought of simply as disobeying God's law in the same way that a person disobeys the laws of a country. Ultimately, the mark sin misses is fellowship with God. The idea that God created humans in his image suggests that we were designed for fellowship with God. Adam and Eve failed to see that the purposes for their lives could only become clear as they maintained their close relationships with God. This was how they missed the mark, and, as Paul suggests in Romans 1—3, all humans make the same mistake. All sinful actions can be reduced to the desire for independence—forging our own destinies without regard for our being created in God's image. Our guilt for breaking fellowship with God must be forgiven, because that is the only way we can begin to restore fellowship. Forgiveness opens up the path to complete restoration.

When ordinary human relationships break down, one or both persons must extend forgiveness in order for the wrongful actions committed to be repaired. To accept forgiveness means to admit that there is something wrong. Forgiveness opens up the possibility for a new relationship to be formed and for growth in that relationship. The same is the case in our relationship with God. When we embrace God's forgiveness, we are admitting we have a problem that only God can fix. This is why forgiveness is the gate of salvation—but it is the *gate* and not the sum total of salvation.

SUMMARY

Viewing sin as a disease helps us understand why holiness and sanctification are crucial to salvation. Both deal with the healing of the person. Although forgiveness of sins is important, it is only the entrance to the larger task of complete healing. Our restoration to God will only be finished when God cures us of the sinful desires that so easily entangle us. God's healing is nothing less than *shalom*—the restoration of harmony within the individual through the quieting of the warfare between the flesh and the Spirit. We anticipate this shalom every Sunday when we see Sunday as the Sabbath, a day of rest designed to help us quiet ourselves before the Lord and rest from our daily struggles. Moreover, shalom does not end with the warfare occurring in the human soul, it extends to every area of life.

The disease of sin permeates every corner of creation. As Paul indicates, all creation groans in anticipation of being set free along with the children of God (Romans 8:21-23). We must allow God to purify us, cleanse us, set us free from sinful desires and heal us. This is the call of the holy life—the life that unfolds before us the moment we turn away from self-destructive choices and turn toward God. In that moment of recognition, God forgives and begins to restore.

ENDNOTES

[1] James D.G. Dunn, *The Theology of Paul the Apostle* (Grand Rapids: Eerdmans, 1998) 114-119.

[2] Luke Timothy Johnson, *Reading Romans: A Literary and Theological Commentary* (New York: Crossroad, 1997) 33.

[3] Johnson, 35ff. where Johnson discusses Paul's argument about Jew and Gentile being in the same condition before God. See also G. Fee, *God's Empowering Presence: The Holy Spirit in the Letters of Paul* (Peabody, MA: Hendrickson, 1994) 489-493. Fee indicates that Paul's answer to both Jew and Gentile is to live by the Spirit.

[4] See *Pelagius's Commentary on St. Paul's Epistle to Romans*, trans. with intro. and notes T. De Bruyn (Oxford: Clarendon, 1993). The dates for Pelagius' life are uncertain. He was exiled in 418 and never heard from again.

[5] I am taking the idea of sin as spiritual pollution from C. Plantinga Jr., *Not the Way It's Supposed to Be: A Breviary of Sin* (Grand Rapids: Eerdmans, 1995) 39-51.

[6] See Dunn, 111-114, for a discussion of this issue.

[7] Johnson, 113-115. See also Dunn's discussion of sin as desire, which he calls self-indulgence. Dunn, 119-123.

[8] Thomas Aquinas, *Summa Theologiae,* 1a2ae, question 82, article 1 (trans. Fathers of the Dominican Provence in *St. Thomas Aquinas: Summa Theologica*, vol. 2 [Allen, TX: Christian Classics, 1948] 956, 957).

[9] I am taking the distinction between natural desires and acquired desires, or wants and needs, from Mortimer Adler, who uses it to explain Aristotle's view of morality. This distinction helps illustrate what it means to have a sinful nature. See Mortimer J. Adler, *Aristotle for Everybody: Difficult Thought Made Easy* (New York: Macmillan, 1978) 83-91.

CHAPTER 2

Fear Factor

That men may know wisdom and instruction, understand words of insight, receive instruction in wise dealing, righteousness, justice, and equity; that prudence may be given to the simple, knowledge and discretion to the youth—the wise man also may hear and increase in learning, and the man of understanding acquire skill, to understand a proverb and a figure, the words of the wise and their riddles. The fear of the Lord is the beginning of knowledge; fools despise wisdom and instruction (Proverbs 1:2-7, *RSV*).

I can still vividly recall the church service in which I committed my life to Christ. During a series of revival meetings at our church, the evangelist preached on hell and the wrath of God. He pounded the pulpit, warning us repeatedly of the dangers of life and death without God. At the conclusion of the sermon, he made a plea for all the teenagers to make a choice. He asked us to stand up and said, "If you want to go to heaven, come down to the front of the church."

He warned us that if we sat down, we were saying to God and the entire congregation that we wanted to go to hell. You can imagine the kind of response he received. No one wants to go to hell and no teenager wants to proclaim to a group of people, "I want all of you to know that I want to go to hell." The result was that every teenager headed to the altar, including me.

I prayed as hard as I could for God to save me. Although I had grown up in church, I had never made a firm commitment to God. After praying, I stood up with the feeling that I was still in trouble with God. The next Sunday, I returned to the altar and pleaded with God to save me from hell and let me into heaven. This happened about five or six times over the course of several weeks. I was terrified that God would send me to hell, and I wanted some kind of assurance that I was really OK. It was years later, while I was attending seminary, that I finally received the assurance I needed.

Fear is a powerful motivator. The evangelist at my church used the fear of eternal torment to move me in the right direction. The problem was, my fear did not go away. The evangelist had painted a portrait of God as a divine and wrathful judge who would not hesitate to send people to hell. This was etched in my mind. Even after I became a Christian, I was concerned that one wrong move could take away my salvation. Not wanting to lose God's blessing or my place in heaven, I worked hard at living right.

At first, my primary motive for living right was the fear of divine punishment, and my primary aim was entrance into heaven. Just like any other phobia, I was afraid of hell and, as a result, afraid of God. It took me years to work through the "fear factor" in my life and the bad theology that caused it. Only after I was able to change my view of God did I begin to understand why He demands holiness from us. Today, fear still functions as a motivator for me, but it's not the kind of terror I felt as a teenager and young adult.

Before we move any further in our discussion of holiness, let's deal with the "fear factor" and the bad theologies that produce it. We also need to understand the right way to fear God and how fear functions as a positive force to lead us toward God, not away from Him. Unless we remove certain perceptions about fear, we will not understand the purpose of holiness.

FEAR AND BAD THEOLOGIES

Two types of erroneous theology give rise to unhealthy fear. When these two theologies are in operation, they can have a paralyzing effect on a Christian's walk. The first is *worm theology* and the second, *light-switch theology*.

Worm theology is the idea that believers should always see themselves as miserable creatures before God, no better than worms. This theology was popularized in the 1700s and promoted through revivalist preaching. To move people to an altar, many evangelists—past and present—have emphasized the idea that people are nothing but worms who deserve harsh judgment. They do not allow the Holy Spirit to bring a person to repentance, but heap guilt and condemnation on him or her by depicting God as a Judge who will not hesitate to send someone to everlasting punishment and condemning every person as thoroughly sinful and deserving of divine wrath. The suggestion that people are worms before God has been used to compel even the strongest Christians to view themselves as wretched sinners.

This is the approach the old hymn writer, Isaac Watts, used in "Alas! And Did My Savior Bleed?" (1707). The first verse says:

> Alas! and did my Savior bleed?
> And did my Sovereign die?
> Would He devote that sacred head
> For such a worm as I?"

Most hymnals today follow the version modified by Ralph Hudson in 1885, which changed the line "For such a worm as I" to "For sinners such as I" and was renamed "At the Cross."

As part of its overemphasis on judgment and wrath, worm theology also promotes shame and guilt. This goes beyond godly sorrow for the sins one has committed. Worm theology pushes the idea of godly sorrow to the extreme, forcing a person to dwell on how worthless he or she is. For the adherent to worm theology, God receives the glory only when Christians see themselves as vile sinners who stand condemned.

A good example of how worm theology works is English theologian John Owen's (1616-1683) advice on how Christians should rid themselves of sin. He says that a person should constantly consider God's holy law, reflecting on God's terror and how God will judge every sin. He writes, "Force your lust to face the gospel, not for relief but for further conviction of its guilt. Look to Him whom you have pierced and be in bitterness. Say to your soul, "What have I done? . . . How shall I escape if I neglect such a great salvation?' "[1]

Owen does not want the believer to find relief in the gospel! After these "general considerations" of the depths of sinfulness, Owen directs the believer to focus on specific sins by noting how many times he has broken his promises to God and how close his heart is to being hardened: "Think of how your spiritual life has so often declined, so that your delight in spiritual disciplines, your obedience to His word, and your prayer and meditation have slackened."[2]

These statements were written to Christians who were attempting to live holy and righteous lives. Owen considers the focus on sinfulness crucial if the Christian is to truly put to death all sin. For Owen, only when Christians load their consciences with intense guilt can they begin to rid themselves of sin.[3] There are several problems with this theology.

1. *Worm theology forces believers to view themselves as miserable creatures who deserve condemnation.* The focus is detecting hidden sin, the evil lurking at the door, and all the ways a person does not measure up to God's righteous standard. This intense focus on hatred of sin sometimes spills over into hatred of the sinner. I am a sinner—vile, worthless and deserving of swift punishment. This kind of self-loathing results in a spiritually unhealthy lifestyle in which the primary motive for doing the right thing is an overwhelming fear that God will send you to hell otherwise.

When this approach to theology is combined with legalistic rules and regulations such as has been the case in the past, it can easily damage our Christian walk. I remember one conversation I had with a part-time preacher about my call to the ministry. As we discussed the challenges I might face, the preacher told me what I needed to do was remove the gold chain I wore around my neck. The gold chain, he insisted, prevented God from anointing and using me because, in his opinion, I did not measure up to God's righteous standard. Was he right? Was I a vile sinner by wearing a gold chain? I was terrified of receiving God's judgment, so I examined the areas of my life where I feared I did not measure up. As a result of this constant evaluation, I found it extremely difficult to grow in grace. I began to view myself in a negative light, not as someone created in the image of God, forgiven and being transformed, but as someone who was condemned and worthy of judgment. In short, I was pursuing holiness out of fear of punishment.

2. *Worm theology produces a performance-based rather than a grace-based Christianity.* The only way many Christians can move beyond viewing themselves as worms is by engaging in a Santa Claus approach to Christianity. They keep lists of dos and don'ts and check them twice, hoping to find out whether they are naughty or nice. The list varies from person to person and from church to church. For some, the list includes reading the entire Bible every year, while for others, it is having a daily quiet time.

Still others think it means being at church every time the doors open. This list could include not wearing certain kinds of clothes, not watching a certain television show, or not listening to certain types of music. This Santa Claus approach compiles a "holiness list" and uses it to evaluate a Christian's performance.

Performance-based Christianity tends toward one of two extremes. We call those who think they faithfully keep their list *condemners*, because they tend to be the first to cast judgment. These Christians complain when someone else gets blessed instead of them. They wonder why God hasn't seen their good behavior and bestowed the blessing on them. You can hear them say something like, "God, I've prayed regularly and I've attended church every time the doors were open, so why have You blessed so-and-so and not me?"

The second type of performance-based Christians tends toward the opposite extreme. We'll call them *the condemned* because they focus on their shortcomings; they fail to keep their list and tend to live under condemnation and fear of God's punishment.

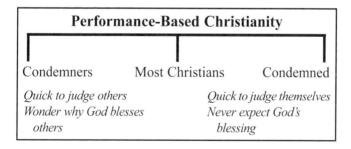

Performance-Based Christianity		
Condemners	Most Christians	Condemned
Quick to judge others		*Quick to judge themselves*
Wonder why God blesses others		*Never expect God's blessing*

Both types of performance-based Christians live with fear that they don't measure up. Condemners choose to focus on the shortcomings of others, while the condemned focus on themselves. Most performance-based Christians are somewhere between the two extremes.

The second bad theology is *light-switch theology*. This theology refers to the idea that one can jump in and out of salvation as easily as switching a light on and off. The implication is that one slip or one wrong move can instantly reverse salvation. This theology comes in all shapes and sizes because most believers have different ideas about what constitutes a wrong move. For example, some Christians think that missing one church service without a good excuse jeopardizes their status with God. As a result of this theology, believers constantly think they must start over in their walk with God because they are always slipping up.

You can detect light-switch theology at work in a church whose members question the state of each other's salvation. Instead of the church being a hospital of grace where people are healed and transformed, it becomes a place where cruel judgment and criticism destroy lives. A more subtle version of this theology is the statement "He's not in God's will." I remember one church member suggesting that his pastor was not in God's will simply because he was not doing things the way this member thought they should be done.

Light-switch theology hinders the Christian walk. When Christians constantly question whether they are in or out of God's will and they struggle to maintain their holiness codes, they begin to think, *Maybe God's allowing this to happen to me because I'm not praying as much this week as I should.* They assume that God is handing out some kind of judgment upon them for their failure to maintain righteous behavior.

When these two theologies combine, it is easy to see the damage they create. Worm theology views God as a wrathful Judge and the person as a vile sinner. Light-switch theology suggests that Christians are always one step away from judgment and in jeopardy of losing their place in God's kingdom.

While many preachers think worm theology and light-switch theology promote holiness, they actually have the opposite effect. Why? Because these erroneous theologies lead to the misguided belief that holiness is a set of rules and regulations that must be kept in order to escape hell and enter heaven. What lies at the center of both worm theology and light-switch theology is the same kind of fear I felt that night I ran toward the altar. This kind of fear is best described as being terrified of divine punishment. It does not create a strong relationship with God, but actually puts distance between God and the believer. Just as individuals flee from a dictator because they do not want to be punished, so adherents to these theologies tend to flee from God.

THE BEGINNING OF WISDOM

Fear of God need not be equated with guilt, divine wrath and judgment. Rather, fear of God evokes the healthy respect humans should have for God, given the difference between God and creation. However, it is more than a healthy respect for God.

As a parent, I certainly want my daughter to respect me, but I do not want her to be in awe of me. After all, even though I am her father, I am a mere human, just as she is a human. The difference between my daughter and me is in our relationship to one another. Respect for God is different. A healthy respect for God includes being in awe of God, because God is a perfect being, not just another human being.

Many people use the word *awesome* to refer to someone or something that is great. You may have heard someone say, "That is awesome!" Usually, the person means that he or she is amazed at what has happened. The term *awesome* is so overused that it has lost most of its original meaning. *Awesome* actually refers to an experience that inspires awe. The term *awe* itself denotes a kind of reverential fear of someone or something. I may say, "That is awesome" when I see my new bike for the first time, but what I really mean is something like, "I can't believe I got a new bike!" I am not struck with reverence and fear at the sight of this new bike.

I can almost hear my college students protesting that they would be struck with reverence and fear if it were the right kind of bike. Some bikes, like Schwinns, require that kind of response. But if that is the case, the person probably does not know what it means to be in awe of someone or something.

Let me explain what I mean by appealing to Isaiah's

vision of God. When Isaiah saw God in the Temple, he was struck with awe at the sight. Isaiah was not just thinking, *I can't believe this is God*, as though he could simply run up and touch God in the same way one could touch a bike. While a person might be surprised that he received such a wonderful bike, there is no apprehension in running up to it, jumping on it and peddling away. But, Isaiah certainly felt apprehension before God. Even more than apprehension, Isaiah's feelings hovered between amazement and trepidation, wonder and reverence.

As C.S. Lewis says of Aslan the Lion in his book *The Lion, the Witch, and the Wardrobe*, "He's good, but he's not safe." We certainly cannot tame or domesticate God, and a healthy respect for God keeps this in our minds. By "fear of the Lord" I do not mean that God cannot be trusted, or that we must be terrified of God. This fear is different from the fright associated with phobias. Instead, I mean we should have reverence for Him and His authority. In this sense, fear is closer to awe than it is to horror or terror.

We can further examine the meaning of fear by briefly examining how Proverbs and Ecclesiastes both affirm the fear of the Lord as the beginning of wisdom. In both books, the idea of fearing the Lord plays an important role in defining a person's relationship to God. Proverbs makes two overarching statements about fearing the Lord: "The fear of the Lord is the beginning of knowledge" (1:7) and "The fear of the Lord is the beginning of wisdom" (9:10). It also makes numerous references to the "fear of the Lord" (14:26, 27; 15:16, 33; 16:6; 19:23; 22:4; 23:17; 28:14).

While Ecclesiastes does not mention fear of the Lord as often (only five times), it uses the idea at key points, concluding with "Fear God, and keep his commandments" (7:18; 12:13). In both Proverbs and Ecclesiastes, "fear of the Lord" describes how a person should relate to God in order to achieve success in life.

The question is, what do Proverbs and Ecclesiastes mean by "fear of the Lord"? First, many commentators suggest that the fear of the Lord is a mind-set or attitude that must be cultivated in an individual.[4] This fear is not an emotional response that we would associate with being frightened at a haunted house. Instead, fear of the Lord represents a constant way of life before God.

Second, if it is the beginning of wisdom, the fear of the Lord must involve an outlook or perspective that produces wisdom. In other words, both Proverbs and Ecclesiastes teach us that if we have this attitude, we will gain insight on how we really should live. Since this attitude must be developed over time, it cannot be an emotional response to God, a kind of fearful cowering, as though God were about to unleash judgment. As one commentator puts it, "This is not the kind of fear that walks on eggshells."[5] Neither Proverbs nor Ecclesiastes teaches that the beginning of wisdom is to live one's life being terrified of God, as though He were an evil dictator, handing out judgments based on His whims. God is not like Adolf Hitler, Saddam Hussein or Joseph Stalin.

With this truth in mind, we can begin to look more closely at how Proverbs uses the phrase. The writer of Proverbs claims that fearing the Lord brings "strong confidence" and is a "fountain of life" that keeps one from death (14:26, 27). It also leads to life because it brings contentment and satisfaction (19:23). Just by looking at these few passages, we can be convinced that this is not the kind of fear associated with the terror of swift judgment, which prompts us to run from Him.

Fearing the Lord is closely associated with the idea of trust.[6] To fear the Lord is to trust that He knows the best course for us to follow. Proverbs 29:25 illustrates this point well when it compares fearing humans with trusting in the Lord: "The fear of man brings a snare, but whoever trusts in the Lord shall be safe" (*NKJV*). Proverbs 3:5-7 makes a similar point: "Trust in the Lord with all your heart, and lean not on your own understanding; in all your ways acknowledge Him, and He shall direct your paths. Do not be wise in your own eyes; fear the Lord and depart from evil" (*NKJV*).

There is a close connection between trusting in the Lord and fearing Him. Fearing God brings a strong confidence that leads to life because it confides ("places faith or trust") in Him to show the path to life. True wisdom comes when we trust God, rather than ourselves or others, to reveal the path to life. This is what it means to fear God and this is how fearing Him is "instruction in wisdom" (15:33). Consequently, Proverbs defines the fear of the Lord like this: Trust in the Lord, who knows all things and will lead you down the right paths.

If we examine Ecclesiastes, we gain a slightly different sense of what it means to fear the Lord. One of the primary aims of the book is to investigate the seemingly purposeless nature of life. The writer is in search of a meaningful life, a life that is not in vain. As he puts it, "All is vanity. What profit has a man from all his labor in which he toils under the sun?" (1:2, 3, *NKJV*). The search for an answer causes the author to ask tough questions:

1. Why do the wicked prosper as much as, if not more than, the righteous? (8:14).

2. Why does God allow someone to become wealthy and prosperous, and then allow his wealth to be taken from him, so that he has nothing? (6:1, 2).

3. Why are so many people oppressed? It would seem better if they had not been born (4:1-3).

Ultimately, the writer concludes that God's ways are mysterious: "As you do not know what is the way of the wind . . . so you do not know the works of God who makes everything" (11:5, *NKJV*).

There are times when this truth hits home, and it usually occurs in the midst of tragedy or an intense struggle. During those times, we become acutely aware that God's purpose for our life remains hidden and difficult to discern. While we have an idea of God's purpose, we recognize that there is still much we do not know.

How, then, do we find meaning amid such apparent vanity and futility? One answer Ecclesiastes gives is to fear God. When we cannot penetrate God's purposes for a tragedy, we must endure the season of life we're in and have reverential respect for God. Fear of God reminds the individual that he or she is a creature, not the Creator. As Ecclesiastes puts it, "No one can find out the work that God does from beginning to end" (3:11, *NKJV*). Although you can discern the seasons of the year, that does not put you in the position of discerning all of God's purposes. The fear of God helps humans remember that they are creatures who must stand in awe before the mystery of their Creator.

Another reference to trust is found in the writer's admonition to fear God. However, this is not a blind trust that confesses to know nothing about God. Ecclesiastes focuses on rejoicing in the gifts God has given, which include wisdom, knowledge, food, drink and joy itself (2:24-26; 3:12, 13; 5:18-20; 8:15).

Based on the New Testament, we could extend the list of God's gifts to include all the blessings of life in Christ. However, Ecclesiastes suggests that even with all of God's gifts, the difference between the foolish and the wise person or the righteous person and the sinner, is not based on the events in their lives. Both experience tragedy, both can have wealth, both can be oppressed and both die (9:2). Rather, the difference lies in their *approach* to the events of life.

The righteous live their lives in relation to God. This defines their character, and enables them to enjoy life's pleasures and endure life's disappointments. Unlike the fool, the wise and righteous person defines his or her well-being not in terms of how long he lives or how much she accumulates, but in terms of the divine character he or she develops that brings joy now and in eternity.[7] This understanding of what it means to flourish grows out of the more fundamental idea of reverence, or fear, for God as Creator. Reverence for the Creator inspires a trust that the same God who gives good gifts has a final purpose that will be realized, even if it cannot be immediately discerned.

WHO IS THIS LORD WE ARE TO FEAR?

There is a connection between what it means to fear the Lord and our concept of God. Those who view this fear as the kind of terror normally associated with phobias tend to view God as a kind of resident policeman or divine judge, waiting to pronounce a sentence on the sinner. This is where worm theology and light-switch theology bear their fruit, producing a theological poison that has disastrous consequences for a believer's relationship with God. These theologies teach that communion with God depends on viewing oneself as a guilty sinner, whose every mistake calls down divine judgment. Herein lies the trap of legalism, in which acceptance by God requires maintaining a certain standard of behavior. While the standard may differ from person to person, there is an emphasis on God as divine judge who can be appeased only when the person acts in certain ways. Servile fear (the fear a servant has of being whipped by his master) and guilt become the driving forces in this relationship, robbing the believer of any joy, because he or she cannot move beyond seeing himself or herself as a sinner (or worm) who stands in judgment.

John Bunyan, author of *Pilgrim's Progress*, tells a story that helps us see how servile fear and a harsh view of God tend to go together.[8] One particular Sunday, Bunyan heard a sermon on the necessity of observing Sunday as a day of rest dedicated to the Lord. The preacher went on to suggest that playing sports or games and working on Sunday were great evils. Bunyan left the church that day feeling quite guilty for his failure to observe the Sabbath as he should. The preacher's sermon led to a battle in Bunyan's mind that played itself out over the rest of the day.

After eating his afternoon meal, Bunyan indicates that he felt better and, ignoring the sermon, decided to play a game. While playing the game "a voice did suddenly dart from heaven into my soul, which said, 'Wilt thou leave thy sins and go to heaven, or have thy sins and go to hell?' At this . . . I looked up to heaven, and it was as if I had . . . seen the Lord Jesus looking down upon me, as being very hotly displeased with me, and as if He did severely threaten me with some grievous punishment for these and other my ungodly practices."

When this thought entered Bunyan's mind, it led him to draw two conclusions:

1. He was the chief of sinners and forgiveness was impossible.

2. If God would damn him if he continued to play the game and damn him if he did not continue, then why not simply continue to sin?

By his own admission, his despair over never being forgiven led him to desire to sin even more, because he saw sinning as the only refuge from the guilt and condemnation he felt. Psychologists have described this behavior as a self-fulfilling prophecy. If a person becomes convinced that everyone thinks he is a horrible sinner, then his response may be to behave exactly that way. It is amazing to consider that, in one afternoon, Bunyan had lost the hope of being forgiven because he saw himself as a sinner about to be severely judged by a wrathful God.

It is important to remember that Bunyan felt guilty for playing a game on Sunday—not for murder, adultery or some other weighty sin. One can see in Bunyan's story the cycle of sin, guilt and forgiveness that forms the legalistic universe. At the center of this universe around which all these things revolve is a misconception of God. As J.B. Phillips suggests, we must see the idea of God as a resident policeman as the unreal picture it is.[9] God is not a cold and wrathful deity who is quick to make rash decisions or who is prone to outbursts of anger.

This false portrait of God creates other misguided ideas about salvation and the purpose of holy living. Before I was a Christian, and even after I became one, I always thought that salvation was about escaping hell and getting into heaven—that seemed to be its primary purpose. Holiness was what God required of someone in order to get into heaven, and in this way, it was part of salvation. I must confess that I did not always know why God required certain actions of me, other than God deciding I must prove my level of commitment to Him. Consequently, my initial motive for living a holy life was fear of hell and desire for heaven. When one considers that as the standard of holiness, the test of commitment keeps getting higher and higher, and it is easy to see how the universe of legalism comes into existence. Like John Bunyan before me, I was caught in a cycle where a piece of jewelry, not reading my allotted five chapters from Scripture, or listening to a certain kind of music led to guilt, fear of hell, and removal of God's blessing (divine judgment).

This view of salvation and holiness leads some people to think that living a holy life is the opposite of happiness. They see themselves as having two choices: live a holy life now and delay happiness until you get to heaven, or take your happiness now and forfeit it later. This is a false dilemma. Holiness is more than fulfilling the necessary prerequisites for getting into heaven. To understand this requires a rethinking of the false portrait of God created by the fear factor of bad theologies.

When Jesus says, "Be perfect, therefore, as your heavenly Father is perfect" (Matthew 5:48), He is not only telling us something we must become, but something that God already is: perfect. When we add James' statement that, in God, "there is no variation or shadow due to change" (1:17), the conclusion seems clear: God is perfect and remains perfect. In fact, God is absolute perfection. The question is, what does it mean for God to be absolute perfection? A theologian from the 12th century, Anselm of Canterbury, helps us answer this question by suggesting that if God is perfect, then He must be anything it is better to be than not to be.[10]

If it is better for God to be all-powerful than to lack power, then He must be omnipotent. If it is better for God to be all-knowing than to lack knowledge, then He must be omniscient. If it is better for God to be completely good than to be evil, then He must be perfectly holy. God must also be perfectly joyful and perfectly happy. When we combine these attributes of God, we see that He is perfectly holy *and* happy.

These two attributes must have something to do with one another. Perfect holiness *is* perfect happiness. God calls us to be like Him—a being that is both perfectly holy and perfectly happy. Consequently, the path of holiness *is* the path to happiness. We cannot have one without the other.

To illustrate this point, we need to recall the example of the man in chapter 1 who committed adultery. Once we see the damage that adultery does to the man, his wife and children, we understand why God says, "Don't commit adultery" (see Exodus 20:14; Deuteronomy 5:18; Matthew 5:27-30). God does not forbid people from committing adultery because He wants to deprive them of fun. Nor is this some arbitrary test God constructs to ensure the faithfulness of individuals to Him. Instead, there is a connection between not committing adultery and being happy in the same way that there is a connection between holiness and happiness. God wants people to have fun while keeping them from engaging in actions that destroy themselves and others.

The same point can be made about sexual practices in general. The moral principle of abstaining from sex outside of marriage is not about restricting the amount of pleasure or fun individuals can have. It is about protecting people from destructive practices that can produce unwanted pregnancies, lead to emotional scarring and hinder healthy sexual relationships in the future.

I have a friend who had sex with multiple partners during high school. Along with these sexual encounters, he repeatedly viewed pornography, with its two-dimensional portraits of women as objects to be used for personal pleasure and instant gratification. In his senior year, he became a Christian and believed God called him into the ministry. He thought he should prepare to fulfill God's calling as best he could, so he decided to attend a Christian college.

While in college, he began to date his future wife. He discovered during their courtship that all of his sexual encounters in high school and his exposure to pornographic materials had shaped the way he perceived women and his past was preventing him from having a healthy relationship. By his own admission, he could not see all of her wonderful qualities because his previous behavior had conditioned him to treat women as objects by valuing only the physical characteristics they possessed. He once exclaimed, "God, she can't be the one: her breasts aren't big enough!" With God's help, he had to reverse the twisted mind-set created by just a few years of engaging in illicit sexual

actions and learn the appropriate way to treat women.
Only after moving beyond the fantasized world created by pornographic images was he prepared to handle
the mountains and valleys that are the joy of marriage.
Abstaining from sex outside of marriage protects individuals from actions that are not good for them or their
future spouses.

SUMMARY

Holiness is not a set of arbitrary commands designed
to test our loyalty to God. He calls us to holiness
because He knows that if we are to be happy, then we
must be holy. Holiness and happiness are part of the
perfect being of God. They are not separate from one
another, but are intimately bound together. This implies
that the path *of* holiness is the path *to* happiness: the
good life. *True* fear of the Lord is the beginning of wisdom because it recognizes that God is our Creator, and
He knows best what makes His creation happy.

Up to this point, I have talked about holiness as
leading to fun, but it is about much more than this—it
is about having the good life, the life that flourishes
and prospers. In addition, while we stand in awe of
God as a perfect being, we should not cower before
Him in terror. God is not a policeman waiting for us to
make a wrong move so He can slap the cuffs on us and
send us off to a place of torment.

To pursue holiness with intense passion, we must
move beyond this false portrait of God and the kind of
servile fear it produces. Our teaching and preaching

should focus on a loving God who demands holiness because He knows it is the only way to flourish and prosper as a human being. The implication of this idea, of course, is that sanctification lies at the heart of salvation and cannot be seen as an "add-on" after conversion.

ENDNOTES

[1] John Owen, *Sin and Temptation: The Challenge to Personal Godliness*, abridged and introduced by J.M. Houston, introduction by J.I. Packer (Portland, OR: Multnomah, 1983) 175.

[2] Owen, 175, 176.

[3] For more on John Owen's views, see the discussion by Sinclair Ferguson in his book *John Owen on the Christian Life* (Edinburgh: The Banner of Truth Trust, 1987) 125-153.

[4] See William P. Brown, *Character in Crisis: A Fresh Approach to the Wisdom Literature of the Old Testament* (Grand Rapids: Eerdmans, 1996) 28, 29, 143-147; R.E. Clements, *Wisdom in Theology: The Didsbury Lectures*, 1989 (Grand Rapids: Eerdmans, 1992) 60-64; and Claus Westermann, *Roots of Wisdom: The Oldest Proverbs of Israel and Other Peoples*, trans. J. Daryl Charles (Louisville, KY: Wesminster John Knox, 1995) 128-130.

[5] Brown, 29.

[6] See Westermann, 129.

[7] Brown, 146, 147.

[8] John Bunyan, *Grace Abounding to the Chief of Sinners* (New York: Penguin Classics, 1987).

[9] J.B. Phillips, *Your God Is Too Small* (New York: Macmillan, 1965) 15ff.

[10] Anselm of Canterbury, *Proslogion*.

CHAPTER 3

Sanctification: The Heart of Salvation

One thing I asked of the Lord, that will I seek after: to live in the house of the Lord all the days of my life, to behold the beauty of the Lord, and to inquire in his temple (Psalm 27:4).

Many Christians equate salvation with forgiveness of sins because they are primarily concerned about getting into heaven. This understanding of salvation shapes how Christians view holiness. When associated with "just making it in," the word *holiness* conjures up ideas about following a set of laws or regulations as the means of maintaining moral purity before God without which a person could not enter heaven. The ultimate point of following these regulations would be to remain in God's favor. Such a view of salvation usually gives rise to the worm and light-switch theologies discussed in the previous chapter.

This approach misses the larger purpose of salvation: transformation of the person into a child of God so that she can reach her complete potential in union and fellowship with God. By reducing salvation to entering heaven and escaping hell, holiness becomes more a test of one's loyalty to God rather than a real transformation.

Is holiness about demonstrating loyalty to God? Is it a series of tests we must pass? Or is it something else? How should we think about holiness and sanctification? What is their ultimate purpose? By answering these questions, I hope we will begin to see how sanctification is the heart of salvation.

ADOPTION: *REAL* SONS AND DAUGHTERS

Let's begin by looking at Paul's use of the word *adoption* to describe salvation:

> But when the fullness of time had come, God sent his Son, born of a woman, born under the law, in order to redeem those who were under the law, so that we might receive adoption as children. And because you are children, God has sent the Spirit of his Son into our hearts, crying, "Abba! Father!" (Galatians 4:4-6).

In this passage, Paul provides a summary of the work of Christ and the Spirit in making believers children of God. He intentionally uses the same verb to describe what God is doing through each. God is *sending* His Son and the Spirit of His Son to bring about our adoption.[1] The parallelism between the Son and the Spirit is clear when one places the verses side by side.

God *sent* his Son
   born of a woman
   born under the law

> to redeem those under the law
> that we might receive adoption as sons
> God *sent* the Spirit of his Son in our hearts
> because we are sons
> crying out, "Abba, Father!"

In this brief passage, Paul describes the work of Christ on the Cross and the work of the Spirit in the heart as the two sides of salvation. Both elements are necessary for adoption. The death of Christ "redeems" humanity from slavery to the disease of sin. It is freedom from a way of living that is self-destructive and brings death. When we become joint heirs with Christ, we leave behind the bonds of slavery and enter into new life as God's children. The freedom of the children of God is receiving the freedom of the Son of God.

As we participate in Christ's death, we enter into a new way of living in which we experience true liberty. For Paul, this liberation is an *experience* because we cry out, "God, you are my Father!" by the Spirit of His Son, sent to confirm our adoption. Those who experience the Spirit of God also experience life in the Son.

Imagine an orphan being adopted into a family and experiencing the warmth of love and acceptance for the first time. She ceases to be an outcast, an object of scorn to be mistreated and to mistreat others, but now forms part of a new family structure. Through Christ and the Spirit, each believer is adopted into the family of God and experiences the liberty of a new family life.

While, in an important way, the adoption of believers is complete, there is another sense in which it still must be completed. Adoption is complete because, through Christ and the Spirit, each person is made part of the family of God. But there is another step. Paul does not conclude his discussion with this dimension of adoption. Instead, he asserts that what now matters for the adopted child is "faith working through love" (Galatians 5:6, *NKJV*), which he will later identify as "walking in the Spirit" (vv. 16-26, *NKJV*).

Adoption into the family of God opens up a new way of life that must be fully actualized. The complete freedom of the sons and daughters of God is found only in complete liberty from the desires of the flesh. As Gordon Fee suggests, when Paul mentions desires of the flesh he is referring to "the basic perspective of life in the flesh." [2]

In light of chapter 1, we could say that the Spirit is at work in believers, liberating them from patterns of thinking and behaving that will destroy. The basic perspective of life in the flesh, or what John's Gospel calls *the world*, enslaves people. If the "adopted" sons and daughters of God are to realize their complete freedom from the world's slavery, they must walk in the Spirit. This is the only way to fully complete adoption into the family of God because only the Spirit can form Christ in them and make them like Christ.

These two aspects of adoption might be better understood if we consider how adoption works today. In modern society, adoption usually includes two phases. In the first phase, the parents apply to adopt a child and sort through the legal matters pertaining to the adoption. This phase is a necessary step to guarantee that the adopted child legally belongs to the parents and has a rightful claim to be an heir. Even if the child is adopted into a family that already has natural children, he should have some legal claim to his parents' estate upon their deaths.

Upon completion of the legal phase, the child becomes a legal heir, entitled to everything his parents possess. In one sense, Paul calls believers *adopted children of God* because he wants to emphasize that they belong to God and are entitled to all God has. For Paul, this adoption is through the Sonship of Christ and is experienced through the Spirit dwelling in our hearts.

The Spirit is God's "down payment" on our lives so that we become joint heirs with His Son, Jesus Christ. Christ is the natural Son of God, while we are adopted sons and daughters of God. Because we are united to Christ, the eternal Son, by the Holy Spirit, we share in Christ's Sonship and become joint heirs with Him.

The legal phase must give way to the second phase, which concerns fully forming the new relationship that has been created. We could call this formation of a new relationship the relational phase, since it speaks to what the child and the parents must now do. Being adopted into a family means that the child must adjust to the new family life as the family adjusts to the child. The child must learn to love his new parents as they learn to love him. This is especially the case with orphans who are adopted at an older age. Once the legal phase is complete, an orphan is no longer parentless and can

truly say for the first time, "You're my mom and dad."
When an orphan calls his parents "Mom" and "Dad"
for the first time, it represents a new commitment on
his part to be a member of this family. However, he
still does not *fully* love his parents. He is their *legal*
son, but he must become their *real* son, which requires
working hard to form this new relationship. A legal
son is entitled to all that a natural child has, including
the privilege to call his parents "Mom" and "Dad." He
has this new privilege because a husband and wife
have chosen to make him part of their family.

What if the son did not seek to develop a relationship with his new parents? In the eyes of the court, he
would still be their son, but without the relational
bonds of love, any legal bond would be meaningless.

To become their son in the fullest sense, he has to
develop the new relationship. This requires that he
change, grow and be transformed. He must adapt to
life with this new family and truly learn to love his
parents. It is only as the relationship grows and develops that he can say with all of the comfort and assurance of a child, "I love you, Mom and Dad, and I trust
your decisions about my welfare."

At some point during their lives, most children have
a sudden realization that they are more like their parents
than they would care to admit. They realize how much
of their lives has been transformed by their parents'
influence. This was certainly the case with me.

The characteristics of my father and mother have
become part of my own characteristics. My father loves

to have something sweet after a meal—even a small taste will do. Like him, I find myself desiring that same sugary taste. I also share the same sentimentality as my father. He cries very easily and items conjure nostalgic feelings for him when others only see junk. I fight his battles, wrestling in my soul with the doubt and despair I so often saw him contending against.

Although I think I share more qualities with my father, my mother's influence is never far away. I share her preference for indoor comforts and the warmth of a bed rather than the outdoors and the floor of a tent like my father. Like her, I could never understand why my father would buy an old vehicle and spend large amounts of money keeping it in "good" condition instead of purchasing something new. Yes, I now realize how alike my parents and I really are and how much of their characteristics were passed on to me and have become my characteristics. As I adapted to life in their home, my behavior and beliefs changed.

My brother is also an incorporation of various elements from our parents. He has my mother's quiet strength and stamina, choosing to fight his battles in the closet of his mind, rather than sharing them with others. Like her, he seldom reveals his true feelings. He has her love for simplicity of lifestyle, taking pleasure in the small comforts that come occasionally.

My brother and I have become microcosms of our parents' personalities. While these characteristics have been shaped by our own personalities, the basic traits remain present and their sources become clearly recognizable upon the slightest investigation. How these characteristics became part of our personalities has always puzzled me, especially since I am adopted and do not share my parents' genetic make-up. The answer lies in the intimate bond developed between parent and child as the child seeks to adjust to life in the new environment. During my formative years, I was imbibing the spirit of my parents, embracing and reacting to their strong influences in my life. I am their *real* son, not merely a *legal* heir to their estate, and I have all the character traits to prove it. Through a process of slow transformation, I learned what it meant to love them as I became part of their lives.

The relationship between parent and child illustrates how the legal phase must give way to the relational side of adoption. We receive the qualities and characteristics of God's nature in the intimate bond of family—God's family—of which we are now a part by virtue of our adoption. Within the dynamic of familial give and take, we discover that we begin to develop habits reflective of God's actions. This suggests not only that we receive characteristics from Jesus as the Head of the family, but also from the church, that is, the community constituting the family itself.

My illustration, like all illustrations, breaks down at certain points. God is not an imperfect parent, meaning that our reaction against God's character involves our own rebellion rather than establishing a unique identity. In fact, establishing identity happens when we strive to plunge into a deeper relationship with

God. He wants us to become His *real* sons and daughters by conforming our lives to Him and taking on His life. Becoming like God in holiness is analogous to being like our parents in personality. Sharing characteristics with my father does not mean I *am* my father. We still remain distinct individuals, with unique bundles of traits and characteristics. Likewise, as I take on God's holy character, I do not become God, or even a god, although I do inherit God's own traits.

Ultimately, we are all orphans whom God has adopted out of the world. In adopting us, He is liberating us from the various forms of slavery that the disease of sin brings. We enter our adoption through the work of Christ and the reception of the Spirit in our lives, by which we learn what it means to call God our "Father." However, as we have seen, this is only the first step in a new journey whereby we must *adjust* to a new family life.

As members of God's family, He wants us to move beyond mere *legal* heirs to His kingdom and become His *real* sons and daughters. This is salvation, which requires our complete transformation to a new way of living. It is only at the end of the process that we will become fully conformed to Christ and enter into the full reality of our adoption as sons and daughters.

As Paul says, "We also who have the firstfruits of the Spirit, even we ourselves groan within ourselves, eagerly waiting for the adoption, the redemption of our body" (Romans 8:23, *NKJV*). Salvation is both our initial adoption into the family of God and our fully realizing that adoption over time as we are transformed. When God invites us to be part of His family, He wants to make us His *real* children who take on His traits and show them to the world.

SANCTIFICATION, CONVERSION AND DISCIPLESHIP

To say that God wants to make us real sons and daughters is another way of stating that God is interested in making us disciples—a lengthy process by which we conform our lives to Christ. In fact, we could use the term *disciple* to describe the entirety of the Christian life. Christians are those who attempt to follow Christ in all that they say and do.

A disciple is an apprentice serving under a master craftsman. The master is the person who has reached the peak of his craft. He has become so good at what he does that he needs no more training. In a sense, a master has reached his complete potential. When a person becomes an apprentice, she must learn a new way of doing things and unlearn old patterns of behavior. Slowly, as she implements what her master teaches her, she becomes a master who can begin to teach others.

Consider the great Renaissance painter, Leonardo da Vinci (d. 1519), who is best known for his famous painting, *The Last Supper*. In many respects, da Vinci had completely developed his talents or potential as a painter. Now, imagine becoming an apprentice of da Vinci and learning how to paint from this master. He might say to you that skill at painting is only part of becoming a great painter. You must also change the way you look at the world. He might ask: When you look at that those trees, what do you see? Do you see the colors of the leaves? The way the reds and yellows and browns all blend together to form a rich hue? Do you see the textures in the bark? How in some places the bark is peeling and rough while in other places it is smooth? Do you see? Do you *really* see the trees in all of their glory? To be a painter you must learn to see the colors and textures of the world with clarity.

An apprenticeship with da Vinci would mean learning the skill of moving a brush on a canvas and seeing all shapes, colors and textures of the world. This would require learning to read the lines on the face of an old man—how they reveal the man's deep wisdom and experience of life—and then be able to paint the same characteristics on a canvas.

As with any other apprentice, the amateur painter would have to unlearn one way of viewing the world and learn a new way of looking at it. The student eventually would become a master after learning from da Vinci how to see the world and capture it on the canvas. This is the heart of discipleship. It is about learning a new way of looking at the world and a new way of acting in the world.

When we think of discipleship as an apprenticeship, we see that it is about conversion from one way of life to another. Many view discipleship as what happens after conversion. They see conversion as the starting point for the Christian walk that must be followed by the hard work of becoming a disciple. When Christians talk about being "saved" or "born again," they usually have their initial conversion in mind. Some evangelistic methods have reinforced this understanding of conversion. Although approaches to evangelism are slowly changing, many Christians still consider evangelism as getting someone to convert by praying a prayer. This understanding of evangelism tends to equate salvation with the initial step of faith, and conversion is limited to that first step. By viewing conversion in this way, we miss its connection to discipleship.

Disciples are undergoing continuous conversion and converts are engaged in discipleship. It's not a movement from one to the other, as though conversion and discipleship represent different stages of the Christian life. As Gordon Fee forcefully states,

> Too long the church has understood "conversion" as having only to do with the beginning point. Biblically understood, conversion has to do with making *disciples* of former pagans like ourselves (even if we were born into Christian homes, we need to be "converted" in this sense). Our Lord did not say, "Go and make converts" but "Go and make disciples." In the long run, only disciples are converts.[3]

One of the best places to see the connection between conversion and discipleship is the Sermon on the Mount (Matthew 5—7). Jesus calls His disciples to convert themselves to a new way of living in the world. It is no mistake that Dietrich Bonhoeffer, a Lutheran pastor and theologian, structured his book,

The Cost of Discipleship, around Matthew 5—7. The Sermon on the Mount provided Bonhoeffer with an opportunity to reexamine the nature of salvation from the perspective of Jesus' call to discipleship. For Bonhoeffer, the call to discipleship issued in the Sermon is one of costly grace, not what he called "cheap grace." As he states, "Cheap grace is grace without discipleship, grace without the cross, grace without Jesus Christ, living and incarnate." [4]

Bonhoeffer suggests that costly grace "is the gospel which must be *sought* again and again, the gift which must be *asked* for, the door at which a man must *knock*. Such grace is *costly* because it calls us to follow, and it is *grace* because it calls us to follow *Jesus Christ*. It is costly because it costs a man his life, and it is grace because it gives a man the only true life" (emphasis mine).[5] The entirety of salvation can be reduced to Jesus' one request, "Come, follow Me." This request is a call to enter into a new life of discipleship that demands transformation.

Bonhoeffer goes on to suggest that the call to discipleship is a call to single-minded obedience. Any close examination of the nature of Christian discipleship makes it clear that only a complete transformation through exclusive obedience to Christ will suffice. There can be no separation between faith and obedience as though one preceded the other. "For faith is only real when there is obedience, never without it, and faith only becomes faith in the act of obedience." [6]

In James' words, a faith that does not give birth to

true acts of obedience has no life in it (2:14-26). So radical is Christ's call that there is little room left for innocent bystanders. It is a call to get in, get out or get run over. As Bonhoeffer, who was executed by the Nazis in 1945, puts it, "When Christ calls a man, he bids him come and die." This is true conversion, plain and simple. It is a lifetime of dying to oneself and converting to Christ. Christian discipleship requires a single-minded obedience that brings about a total change.

If we are not careful, all of this talk about discipleship and conversion may cause us to lose sight of Christ's ultimate aim. Entering into an apprenticeship with Christ is not like engaging in any other apprenticeship. Christ is not a mere human being—He is the eternal Son of God. When Christ bids someone to come and die, He also bids him or her to come and live—really live. This is the paradox of Christianity. By dying, we live, and we live only when we die. Disciples of Christ are being transformed into the glorious likeness of the eternal Son of God. They are being healed of the disease of sin, which leads to death, and are coming to possess the abundant life that is only available through Christ. To be completely cured of this disease requires a death to the world's self-destructive way of life and an open embrace to a new way of living that will ultimately lead to eternal life. We must never forget that Christ's call to come and die is *really* a call to come and live. But to live, we must die to patterns of behavior and ways of thinking that bring about our spiritual demise.

Sanctification: The Heart of Salvation

It should begin to be clear why sanctification stands at the center of salvation. Sanctification is certainly about separation from the world's standard of thought and behavior, but God separates us by a slow and steady transformation. Separation from the world is nothing less than a separation from self-destructive patterns of thinking and behaving.

Following the Gospel and letters of John, we could call these negative patterns of behavior *worldly*, as long as we remember that *worldly* refers to behavior that emerges from life without God (see 1 John 2:15-17). As mentioned in chapter 1, this is what results from the dis-ease of sin. Entire communities can be given over to worldly behavior, like racism, that devalues other human beings. We should also not forget that we are all "worldly" to the extent that we engage in destructive behavior that blinds us to the truth. God wants to sepa-rate us, or sanctify us, from those behaviors, because He knows they will destroy us in the end.

God's sanctifying transformation of our lives—His demand for holiness—is really for our good. God is not interested in making us jump through hoops for the sake of watching us jump. No master makes his apprentice do things that are frivolous, even if it may seem that way sometimes. A true master knows that everything he makes his apprentice do is ultimately for the good of the apprentice and will help develop his or her complete potential.

In 1984, a movie was released called *The Karate Kid*. It was about Daniel, a kid who learned karate

79

from a Japanese handyman named Mr. Miyagi. At one point in the training, Mr. Miyagi asked Daniel to wax six cars in his yard using a particular method. Daniel had to put on the wax by moving his left hand counterclockwise and take off the wax by moving his right hand clockwise. Initially, Daniel did not question Mr. Miyagi because he wanted to please his master. But by the end of the day, he decided that he was finished with this pointless task.

He stormed over to Mr. Miyagi and demanded to know why he was waxing cars instead of learning karate. Instead of giving him a direct answer, Mr. Miyagi began throwing punches directly at Daniel. To Daniel's surprise, he was able to deflect the punches by moving his left hand counterclockwise and his right hand clockwise—the exact motions he had been using to wax the cars. What Daniel thought was a frivolous chore turned out to be a karate lesson.

God does not ask us to live holy lives just because He wants to watch us put on and take off certain behaviors. God knows that His call to transformation is a healing call that helps us grow and develop so that we can reach our full potential.

HOLINESS, BEAUTY AND PERFECTION

Up to this point, I have discussed how sanctification relates to becoming complete disciples of Christ through conversion. While conversion is a lengthy process involving our transformation, it is dependent on the divine medicine of Christ and the Spirit. The medicine that comes to us is nothing less than God's own life and power being poured into us.

God sent His Son and Spirit into the world to heal and deliver. Through our adoption into His family, God has become the cure. As we "convert" our lives, we receive God's life and take on His character because we are gradually conformed to the eternal Son of God through the eternal Spirit of God. It is a life of holiness and happiness—the other side of sanctification. It is not simply a separation from self-destructive lifestyles, but a union with God's own life so that we come to reflect that life in all that we do. God desires to bring us into a condition fully reflective of all that He is—a Being whose existence must be described as the beauty of perfection.

We need to see the connection between holiness, beauty and happiness. God's holiness is His beauty and this beauty gives rise to His happiness. When we begin to see holiness as the beauty of perfection we can get a glimpse of what God has for us. We are being transformed from people deformed by the disease of sin to people made beautiful by the grace of God.

In his *Theology of the Old Testament*, Walter Brueggemann discusses the relationship between beauty and holiness.[7] He first points out the connection between the Tabernacle as a place of beauty *and* a place set apart for God. From the description of the Tabernacle in Exodus 25—31, it was to be a place of unsurpassed glory and splendor because it was where God's own glory and splendor would dwell. The gold, the precious stones, the lavish fabrics and the artistic design all pointed toward the magnificence and loveliness of God. This is the pattern that God himself gave to Israel (25:8, 9).

As Brueggemann suggests, this pattern is also reflected in Solomon's construction of the Temple (1 Kings 6:14ff). Solomon spares no expense in building an elaborate structure and furnishing it with the finest woods and metals. And, once again, God's glory comes to dwell in this glorious house (8:10). The designs of the Tabernacle and the Temple tell us something about the nature of holiness. Holiness is not simply being set apart—it concerns *how* we are set apart. Most people focus on being set apart while losing sight of the fact that the way God sets us apart is by calling us to reflect His own beauty in the world. The Tabernacle was set apart as a place of beauty; its beauty reflected God's beauty; its splendor, God's splendor.

God's use of material objects for the Tabernacle and Temple should not cause us to dwell on the objects themselves. It would be a misreading of these texts to think they imply that we must clothe ourselves with fine apparel and jewelry to best demonstrate God's holiness. The gold and precious stones reflect what the Psalmist would later describe as "the beauty of holiness" (29:2; 96:9, *NKJV*).

When he placed the ark of the covenant in the Tabernacle at Jerusalem, David proclaimed to all Israelites that they should "worship the Lord in the beauty of holiness" (1 Chronicles 16:29, *NKJV*).

Brueggemann suggests that the phrase "beauty of holiness" prompts us to see the presence of the Lord as involving a holiness that reflects "symmetry, proportion, order, extravagance, awe, and overwhelmingness." [8] That is, God's holiness is to be found in the beauty arising from the order and harmony at the center of His life. It is the beauty of God's own perfect goodness, where nothing is out of place and all of His actions and thoughts blend together in perfect harmony and move as one in the same righteous direction. This is the one true harmony of Father, Son and Holy Spirit that is to be reflected in the harmony and wholeness (*shalom*) God desires for the world.

Consider for a moment what the disease of sin does to humans. It disfigures us. This happens through the breakdown of relationships on multiple levels. As an inborn and self-inflicted disease, sin is about the breakdown in the harmony and order within us. We are engaged in an interior battle where our natural desires and our acquired desires work against one another. We make self-destructive choices that disfigure our lives and lead down dead-end paths, culminating in death. As a socially-inflicted disease, sin is about the breakdown in the harmony and order within the human family. We do not live at peace with one another or with our environment. Instead, we wound our fellow human beings with our words and deeds. We also destroy our planet by haphazardly consuming its resources. Finally, the disease of sin drives a wedge between us and God. Like a savage addiction to a drug pits a child against his parents, sin rips apart our connection to God. In all of these ways, sin disfigures the beauty of God's Creation by destroying its harmony and order.

Holiness and sanctification are about the restoration of harmony and order so that all we do reflects the perfect goodness of God. To say that God wants to sanctify us means that He wants our lives to display the order and harmony of His life. When we reflect the order and harmony at the center of God's own life, we will be separated from all worldly kinds of behavior. This is how He sets us apart. Like the Tabernacle and the Temple, our lives become places where His glory dwells as they slowly take on the beauty of His perfection.

How can our lives reflect God's beauty? What does it mean to display God's own harmony and order? To understand the point, we need to think about what it means for people to take on a kind of beauty when they are engaged in some activity. Some people do what they do so well that we can see a kind of beauty in their performance. We describe this beauty as "poetry in motion." Have you ever watched someone play a sport so well that you described it as "poetry in motion?" What about a musical performance? Have you watched a pianist play so well that you thought it was "poetry in motion?" What do we mean when we claim to have seen "poetry in motion?"

We usually have in mind the beauty of the performance. Poetry itself has a kind of orderly and harmonious pattern we can detect in its rhymes and rhythms. When we describe a performance as "poetry in motion," we are referring to the order and harmony in the actions. It is the perfect blend of actions in which all parts work together to produce a whole that is greater than the sum of the parts.

Consider the example of a baseball pitcher like Sandy Koufax. When I was younger, I had the privilege of getting Sandy Koufax's autograph at the spring training camp of the Los Angeles Dodgers in Vero Beach, Florida. It was a moment I will never forget, because Sandy Koufax is one of the best pitchers to ever play the game of baseball. One of the greatest moments of Koufax's career was on September 9, 1965, when he pitched the perfect game. In baseball, a no-hitter is remarkable enough. But a pitcher could have a no-hitter and still not pitch a perfect game—he could throw enough balls to walk someone. A perfect game is one of those rare occasions where a pitcher makes no mistakes.

In her review of *Sandy Koufax: A Lefty's Legacy* by Jane Leavy, Teresa DiFalco provides an apt description:

> A perfect game occurs when a pitcher throws nine complete innings with no hits, walks, errors, or base runners. Twenty-seven men walk up to the plate, and twenty-seven men sit down. It may be the most phenomenal athletic feat in all of sports, requiring amazing physical and mental stamina. It is riveting to watch.[9]

The performance is described as "perfect" because it represents the best a pitcher can do. On September 9, Sandy Koufax had reached his complete potential as a pitcher; he pitched the perfect game.

There are other details about Koufax's performance that night which make it even more amazing. For one, he had arthritis in his pitching elbow and was planning on retiring because the pain was so intense. The entire time Koufax was pitching the game free from mistakes, he was in excruciating pain. Secondly, almost by accident, a three-minute film segment of Koufax's pitching was shot by a trainer, because the Dodgers coaches wanted to see Koufax's pitching motion in order to help him. Since the trainer only had three minutes of film, he decided to tape Koufax's pitches only. What appears on the film is Sandy Koufax, throwing pitch after pitch. When she was being interviewed by Terrence Smith on *The MacNeil/Lehrer NewsHour*, Jane Leavy noted that the film revealed how each pitching motion exactly repeated the one before.[10]

According to Leavy, it was this consistent action that made Koufax perfect that night. With every pitch, he was able to repeat the same fluid motion. Koufax struck out 14 batters during the course of the game, which means that he had the same fluid motion at least 42 times. His performance was nothing less than poetry in motion, because each wind-up and pitch involved a rhythmic movement that delivered strike after strike after strike.

Sports players, like Koufax, are given heroic status because they perform feats that are rare. This is why we single them out. They attain a kind of beauty and perfection in their sport others cannot duplicate. On one September evening, Sandy Koufax achieved the beauty of perfection as a baseball pitcher. His performance reached such a level that it far surpassed normal performance, even among professional baseball pitchers. By looking closely at Koufax's performance, we can glimpse the beauty of perfection God wants us to reflect in our lives.

1. *We will reflect God's beauty of perfection when we are able to perform our best.* Koufax pitched the *perfect* game because his performance was the best a pitcher could do. To be sure, he did not arrive at a state of absolute perfection, which only God can possess. The *perfection* we will come to possess is better described as "reaching our complete potential." Koufax had reached his potential as a pitcher. He could go no higher. When we reach our potential as human beings created in God's image, we will enter a kind of perfection. When the image of God is fully developed in such a way that we really do reflect God's life, we will be complete or perfect. This is the kind of perfection God wants us to have. It is a reflection of His absolute perfection because we are doing the best *we* can do, not the best *God* can do.

2. *We will reflect God's beauty of perfection when the mind, will and body work together in order and harmony.* The perfection of Koufax's performance resulted from his ability to focus on reaching one goal: throwing strikes across the plate. There was nothing out of sync that night; no wayward thought leading him astray; no desire pushing him in another direction. Instead, his skill as a pitcher enabled him to focus all

his desires on the same goal. The order and harmony of his performance resulted from the way he organized his thoughts and desires. For a brief period of time, they were working together instead of against one another. He made no "unrighteous" choice because every choice was an example of the right way to deliver a baseball over home plate.

3. *We will reflect God's beauty of perfection when we arrive at true integrity.* None of us has integrity. Why? Because true integrity comes from wholeness and none of us is completely whole yet. The term *integrity* means full, whole or complete. When we talk about someone having integrity, we usually mean that their actions are consistent with what they believe. To put it differently, their beliefs and behaviors are functioning together as a harmonious whole. Their actions reflect the moral demands they believe God has made of them. Sandy Koufax certainly achieved something like this kind of integrity the night he pitched a perfect game. He experienced what it was like to function as a *whole* in which thoughts, desires and choices all worked as one. His pitching aligned itself with his beliefs about the right way to pitch. God always functions as a whole. He never has a wayward thought or desire whereas we always have wayward thoughts and desires. We will possess integrity, when, by God's help, we *integrate* all the various parts of our lives so that they function as a whole. Integrity emerges from complete transformation in which every part of us works together as one.

4. *Separation from the world happens as we slowly come to reflect God's beauty of perfection.* Do you think that anyone watching Sandy Koufax thought of him as just another pitcher? The beauty of Koufax's performance that night separated him from all other professional baseball pitchers. His plaque now hangs in the Baseball Hall of Fame because he was separate, and everyone who knows baseball recognizes that.

This is how God separates Christians from the world. For Christians, it's not about the beauty of pitching, it's about the beauty of a life in which everything is functioning as God intended it to function. What we are striving toward is an order and harmony among our thoughts and desires so that we always choose what is right before God. The closer we come to that kind of performance, the more we take on God's own moral and spiritual beauty. When we perform in that way, it automatically separates us from the world.

While sanctification is about separation from the world, we cannot forget that this separation is a natural result of reflecting the beauty of God's own life. We need not worry about maintaining some sort of conscious distance from everything and everyone. Like Koufax, as we come to reflect the beauty of perfection, everyone will take notice. We will be in the world, but not of the world.

5. *We will reflect God's beauty of perfection when we are fully healed.* Koufax's performance on that night came at the end of a long struggle of learning how to focus his mind. When Koufax first entered

professional baseball, he could not control his pitches. Through constant practice, he had to transform himself from a wild pitcher to one who could consistently throw strikes. He had to remove the defects in his pitching before he could achieve perfection.

God has to remove all of our defects before we fully reflect the beauty of His perfection. Sanctification concerns the gradual removal of the disease of sin through the work of Christ and the Spirit so that one day "this corruptible [will] put on incorruption and this mortality [will] put on immortality" (1 Corinthians 15:53, *NKJV*). When the disease is finally removed in its entirety, then we will be perfect.

SUMMARY

What is the purpose of sanctification or holiness? Is holiness just about demonstrating loyalty to God, or is it more about a real transformation? I believe it is about the latter. God wants to transform us so that we can reflect the beauty of His perfection in our lives. When God adopts us into His family, He invites us to enter into a new way of living that is good for us. He wants *real* sons and daughters who love Him and long to be like Him. Likewise, the radical call to discipleship is really a call to be all that God has created us to be.

When Jesus bids a man to come and die, He is really saying, "Come to me and *live*." We truly come to live when we reflect the beauty of God's own perfection in our lives. This will occur when we arrive at the place where our thoughts and desires no longer work against us, but, as one, push us in the right direction. No doubt, what I am describing requires a long and hard journey. What we must keep in mind is that this is a healing journey whereby we are slowly separated from the self-destructive patterns of behavior that now dominate "the world."

God's call is to be transformed . . . to be healed . . . to be human.

ENDNOTES

[1] See Fee's discussion of this passage from which I am partially drawing. Fee, *God's Empowering Presence*, 398-412.

[2] Fee, 432.

[3] Gordon D. Fee, *Paul, the Spirit and the People of God* (Peabody, MA: Hendrickson, 1996) 75.

[4] Dietrich Bonhoeffer, *The Cost of Discipleship*, second edition, trans. R. H. Fuller (New York, NY: Macmillan Publishing, 1959) 47.

[5] Bonhoeffer, 47.

[6] Bonhoeffer, 69.

[7] Walter Brueggemann, *Theology of the Old Testament: Testimony, Dispute, Advocacy* (Minneapolis, MN: Fortress, 1997) 425-429.

[8] Brueggemann, 427.

[9] Teresa DiFalco, review of *Sandy Koufax: A Lefty's Legacy*, by Jane Leavy, PopMatters Online. <http://www.popmatters.com/books/reviews/s/sandy-koufax.shtml> Retrieved 16 February 2004.

[10] Jane Leavy, "Conversation: *Lefty's Legacy*," interview by Terence Smith, *The NewsHour* October 21, 2002. <http://www.pbs.org/newshour/conversation/July-dec02/leavy_10-21.html> Retrieved 17 February 2004.

PART II:

THE THEOLOGY OF HOLINESS

CHAPTER 4

The Call to Be Human

Do not be ashamed, then, of the testimony about our Lord or of me his prisoner, but join with me in suffering for the gospel, relying on the power of God, who saved us and called us with a holy calling, not according to our works but according to his own purpose and grace. This grace was given to us in Christ Jesus before the ages began, but it has now been revealed through the appearing of our Savior Christ Jesus, who abolished death and brought life and immortality to light through the gospel (2 Timothy 1:8-10).

Most of the time, when Christians discuss the nature and purpose of God's call, they focus on the specific call God has for each person. This idea of calling may be better explained by the word *vocation*, because vocation points to the particular arena in which a person works for God. Sometimes our vocation can be the same as our career choice, but this is not always the case.

Teachers are good examples of those whose careers and vocations go hand in hand. Yet, there are many people who pursue a career in business in order to provide for themselves and their families while also pursuing their vocation. Someone who feels called to minister to the homeless in the inner city may also work at a bank. The former is her vocation and the latter is her career. When we ask the question, "What has God called me to do?," we normally associate it with the specific vocation God wants us to pursue.

While this idea of calling is important, we also need to consider the general call God has given to all human beings: the *calling to fellowship*. Examining calling from this perspective broadens it from the specific arena to which God calls us as individuals to God's purpose for us as members of the human race. Since calling always relates to divine purpose, God's specific vocation refers to His purpose for each individual that relates directly to their sharing as coworkers in His mission of reconciling and restoring the entire world. This specific calling may be designated as God's *calling to witness.*[1] While God calls individuals to be coworkers in His mission to reconcile and restore, he also calls all humans to receive His work of reconciliation and restoration.

God's specific call to pulpit ministry, ministry to the homeless, ministry in a foreign land and so forth, is how individuals share in God's mission to reconcile and restore the entire world. This is the calling to witness. In this sense, Christians become God's agents of reconciliation (cf. 2 Corinthians 5:16-21). However, Christians are also being reconciled and restored while they serve as agents of reconciliation. The restoration of the relationship between God and the individual remains an ongoing process. This is the calling to fellowship. When considering God's general call to all humans, we should think of it as God's call to fulfill one's purpose as a human being, which God brings about by gradually restoring us to full relationship with Himself.

Calling to Fellowship (General Call)
God's purpose for us as human beings
Recipients of Reconciliation
Those being transformed and changed

Calling to Witness (Specific Call)
God's purpose for us as participants in His mission
Agents of reconciliation
Agents of God's transforming grace

To come at this idea from a different perspective, consider what it means to be created in the image of God. God created us in His image, which suggests that He has designed humanity with a purpose. Moreover, this purpose reflects a general calling to be all that He has designed humans to be. Sin may have frustrated His purpose for humanity, but it was not destroyed. If sanctification is the heart of salvation because it is how God seeks to restore His image in human beings, then the call to holiness goes together with the call to be human. Sanctification is the process of being made holy whereby humans are restored to full fellowship with God and enabled to fulfill His original purpose of becoming all He has designed them to be. In other words, only when we complete the process of sanctification and become conformed to Christ do we fully realize our potential as beings created in God's image.

God's call to live a holy life is the same as His call to live a human life. Holiness is God's way of indicating the purpose for humanity by showing us the kind of life He intends us to live. Jesus indicates the kind of life He will give when He declares, "The thief does not come except to steal, and to kill, and to destroy. I have come that they may have life, and that they may have it more abundantly" (John 10:10; *NKJV*). Abundant life is not just eternal life in the sense that we will live forever, it is also our sharing God's triune life, the life of holiness. God created humans in His image with the original intention of enabling them to share in His life. Peter clearly communicates this idea when he indicates that God's divine power enables believers to participate or share in the divine nature (1 Peter 1:3, 4).

As indicated previously, since God is holy and happy, sharing God's life means participating in a kind of life that is abundant, holy and happy. This is the kind of life that flourishes and reaches its complete potential. When this happens, a person comes to reflect the beauty of God's own perfect life and experiences the abundance of that life. This is the general calling God has for the entire human race.

We must understand that pursuing holiness is pursuing abundant life because only then will we find the motivation to make holy choices over the course of our lives. In this chapter, I want to explore the nature and purpose of God's general call to the human race and how it relates to His specific vocation for each individual. I also want to discuss the purpose of the church as

part of God's call to live a holy life. Many people do
not take the need to be part of a church seriously
enough because they do not see the connection
between being part of the body of Christ, being conformed to Christ and flourishing as a Christian. How
can we become conformed to Christ through a holy
life apart from the body of Christ? How can we reach
our full potential in Christ without the admonition and
support of the Christian community? How can we
engage in true discipleship without belonging to a
group of disciples?

In the church, we fulfill our calls to live holy lives
and our vocations to work for God. We begin to live
abundant lives as we become part of the body of Christ,
and in that body we learn how to fulfill God's call to be
holy and work for Him.

THE CALL TO BE HUMAN

God's general call is not trumpeted from the halls of
heaven in the same way that Isaiah's call comes forth
from God's throne (see Isaiah 6). God's general call
does not come with a shout, but a whisper. It is His
hushed whisper into a person's ear that she is ordained
for something more. Humans sense this call deep within the core of their being. They hear the divine whisper
in their dissatisfaction with life. Their restlessness indicates an unsettled sense that there must be more to life.
Augustine (d. 430), a theologian from the early church,
captured this whisper so well when he stated, "You
arouse man that he may delight in praising You

because, O Lord, you have made us for Yourself and our hearts are restless until they rest in Thee." [2] God arouses us at the center of our lives because, as Augustine puts it, He made us for Himself. The divine whisper is simply, "I have made you for Myself."

God's voice is not heard aloud; it comes from within us. If we listen closely, we hear this whisper in our own hearts. "Our hearts are restless," Augustine says. Our desires take us here and there. We yearn for the stuff of life, but we cannot find contentment and satisfaction. While most find small slices of contentment here and gain some satisfaction there, it is never enough. Like tantalizing scraps thrown to the floor, we lick up the delights of this world only to find ourselves more and more hungry. Our desires cannot be satisfied. We are people lost in a foreign land, wandering aimlessly through life and searching for some place to rest. We want to go home—wherever that is. And, that's the moment when we hear it. It's no more than a fleeting impression that there must be more and that your life must have a purpose. It is simply, "I have made you for Myself."

When Christians refer to the "God-shaped hole" at the center of the human heart, they are usually drawing out the idea of being created in God's own image. Augustine knew that God made humanity for Himself because humanity was created in God's image. He also believed that God's whisper could be found in the image. Many theologians, including Augustine, infer the idea of a general call to humans on the basis of their being created in God's image. From the outset, God designed humanity to be like Him, to reflect His own life and to participate in that life. The restlessness humans experience is a direct result of their failure to respond to this general call to be in relationship with God. "Our hearts are restless until they rest in thee."

A brief look at Genesis indicates why theologians associate God's call with the creation of humanity. The text declares,

> And God said, "Let us make man in our image, after our likeness. They shall rule the fish of the sea, the birds of the sky, the cattle, the whole earth, and over every creeping things that creep on the earth." And God created man in His image, in the image of God created He him; male and female He created them (Genesis 1:26, 27).[3]

The fact that God decided to place the stamp of His own life on humanity suggests that there is a fundamental correspondence between them.[4] It is part of God's design that humans be in relationship with Him. From the beginning, humans were created with a bent toward heaven, an openness toward the Creator who fashioned them.[5] Humanity is the one part of Creation in which God can see Himself. Humans mirror God's own life.

How is it that humanity mirrors God? In the past, some theologians have attempted to locate the image of God in some part of humans. They have suggested that humans mirror God because they can reason with their minds. Since no other animal in Creation has the capacity to think in the way humans do, theologians quickly supposed that this must be the way humans reflect God.

While the capacity to think may be one part of the way humans reflect God, a closer look at Genesis suggests that the image cannot be found in a specific place. We should not try to dissect humans in order to discover what exact part makes them like God. Humans simply are the image of God. To be human is to be in the image, and to be in the image is to be human.[6] The image of God is not located somewhere in a person. Instead, it is the whole person and everything about the person. It is like trying to say that what makes a car a car is its engine when there is much more to a car than an engine. An engine is only one part of a car. What makes humanity the image of God is not one part, but the sum total of all the parts. It is important to understand this point because it tells us that the call to be human is a call to be God's image and reflect God's life. We cannot be all God intended us to be—the humans He has created—unless we reflect Him in every area of our lives.

What is it about humanity that makes it the image of God? In a sense, we have already answered this question. God has designed humanity for relationship—relationship with Himself, with one another and with Creation. Each person's mind, will, desires and emotions help foster and sustain these relationships. Notice that the Genesis text places the image of God in male/female relations. "In the image of God He created him; male and female He created them" (v. 27).[7]

Humans most fully reflect God and God's own life as we exist in relationships. Consequently, the image of God corresponds to an inherent capacity for relationship that humans must develop. God not only created humans for Himself, but for one another. While humans were designed for relationship, they must develop those relationships. Even in the Garden of Eden, Adam and Eve had to develop and grow in their relationships with God and one another. It is a mistake to think that Adam and Eve already had everything. What they had was the potential for everything. They had the potential to cultivate their relationships with God and, as they communed with God, they were developing this potential. We could say they were learning what it meant to be in relationship with God, with one another and with Creation. They were learning what it meant to be human.

To suggest that Adam and Eve lacked something does not imply that they were flawed. Humans were created good, but that is not the same as saying they were created with everything. It simply means they were created without any flaws (sin). There were no obstacles hindering Adam and Eve from pursuing their relationships with God and with one another. However, they did have to pursue these relationships. Moreover, this implies that they had to grow and develop. God designed them *for* relationship, but they still had to actively pursue their relationships.

With this in mind, we can see the point of God's command not to eat of the Tree of Knowledge of Good and Evil. God was not testing their loyalty, but calling them to grow in Him by trusting Him even if they could not see the immediate point of trusting Him. Relationships need an environment of trust to grow and flourish. Even after 11 years of marriage, my wife and I must trust each other because we are still learning new things about one another. Our relationship develops and matures through our mutual trust. If we did not trust one another, we could not learn to love one another. Adam and Eve did not have any obstacle keeping them from developing their relationships with God and one another, but they still had to develop them, which means they had to grow and mature.

We should also notice that their growth and development had a purpose. After they sinned, God banished them from the Garden of Eden, lest man "reach out his hand and take also from the tree of life, and eat, and live forever" (Genesis 3:22). The fact that God placed the Tree of Life in the Garden indicates that His plan was to bring humans from mortality to immortality. This plan was to be the culmination of Adam and Eve's own relationships with God. Through their relationships with God and with one another, they were developing to the point where they would eat of the Tree of Life and fully enter into God's own life. It is not by accident that the Book of Revelation places the Tree of Life in the center of New Jerusalem (22:2). God's plan has always been the same. He calls people to realize their complete potentials through Him. The ultimate purpose of being created in God's image is to share His own life, which the Tree of Life exemplifies.

A glance at the Ten Commandments reinforces the idea that humans were designed for relationship. As the heart of God's law, the Ten Commandments provide a summary of the two great commandments: Love God and love neighbor. What we see in the Ten Commandments is God's attempt to remind humans that they exist for Him (love God) and for one another (love neighbor).

Relationship to God (Loving God)	Relationship to Others (Loving Neighbor)
1. No other gods.	5. Honor your parents. (Respect authority.)
2. No idols.	6. No murder. (Respect life.)
3. No wrongful use of God's name.	7. No adultery. (Respect marriage.)
4. Remember the Sabbath.	8. No theft. (Respect property.)
	9. No false witness. (Respect truth.)
	10. No coveting. (Respect friendship.)

When sin entered the world, it broke down these relationships in fundamental ways. Sin corrupts God's original design. Humans were to flourish as they reflected God's own life in and through their relationships with one another. The Ten Commandments are God's reminder that the way to flourish is by restoring proper relationships.

We understand why God designed humans for relationship when we consider what it means for God to exist as Father, Son and Holy Spirit. God exists as a Trinity of persons. He is one God, eternally existing in three persons: the Father, the Son and the Holy Spirit.[8]

At the center of God's life, we find a relationship between three divine persons. God exists in relationship. If God is triune and God is love, then Father, Son and Holy Spirit all exist in a communion of love, each giving and receiving love.

When God created humans in His image, He called them to reflect the pattern of His own life. This life is abundant because it is filled with the joy and happiness bursting forth from the giving and receiving of love by Father, Son and Holy Spirit. Remember, the beauty of God's own life can be found in the one true harmony of Father, Son and Holy Spirit. God is absolute perfection *because* He exists in triune relationship and calls us to reflect that perfection through our relationships with Him and with one another.

Having examined what it means to be created in the image of God, we can begin to glimpse the general call to fellowship. From the outset, God has designed humans to be in relationship with Him and to share His life. Although God created Adam and Eve without any flaws, He still expected them to pursue and develop their relationships with Him and with one another. Indeed, this is how all humans reach their complete potential. The road to fellowship with God is much more difficult now that the disease of sin infects humanity. In fact, it is impossible for humans to develop their complete potential apart from being healed by God. To enable humans to flourish in and through a relationship with Him, God must lead us on an exodus out of sin and death—He must re-create humanity.

CHRIST, THE SPIRIT AND NEW HUMANITY

It is no mistake that Christ is the "image of the invisible God" (Colossians 1:15) and the Savior of humanity at the same time. Who better to bring God's image in humanity to completion than the One who is "the exact imprint of God's very being" (Hebrews 1:3)? The life, death and resurrection of Christ show that He was chosen to lead humanity out of sin and death. When we want to find a example of what it means to be a real human being, one in whom the image of God is seen most clearly, we need look no further than Jesus of Nazareth. He is true humanity in all of its glory.

The New Testament uses a variety of expressions to indicate that God in Christ is creating a new humanity who will fully reflect all that He is. In the Book of Hebrews, Christ is the pioneer, or captain, of our salvation (2:10; 6:20; 12:2). The way God decided to bring many sons and daughters to glory was "to make the captain of their salvation perfect through sufferings" (2:10, *NKJV*). Jesus is also the "pioneer [captain, author] and perfecter of our faith" (12:2, *NKJV*). Taken together, these two passages suggest that Jesus initiates our salvation by showing us how to perfect our own faith through trusting God entirely in the midst of sufferings.[9] Jesus is also our captain in the sense that He alone opens the way to God and makes our restoration possible. This eternal Son, who is the radiance of God's own glory and bears the stamp of God's essence (1:3), is the One sent into the world to lead humanity out of the darkness of its own condition.

While the author of Hebrews chooses the language of *captain* or *pioneer*, Paul describes Jesus as the *Second Adam*, or the firstfruits of a new way of life (Romans 5:12-21; 1 Corinthians 15:20-23, 45-49). As John Ziesler notes, when Paul contrasts Adam with Christ, he is describing two different ways of being human.[10] Whereas Adam failed and introduced sin and death to the world, Christ succeeded and brought about righteousness and peace. "For as by one man's disobedience many were made sinners, so also by one Man's obedience many will be made righteous" (Romans 5:19, *NKJV*). Moreover, the new exodus Christ brings culminates in the resurrection of our bodies.

Once again, Paul employs the contrast between Adam and Christ to make his point: "And so it is written, 'The first man Adam became a living being.' The last Adam became a life-giving spirit" (1 Corinthians 15:45, *NKJV*). Drawing on Genesis 2:7, where God is said to have breathed the breath of life into Adam, Paul claims that the resurrection body of Christ is not simply life-receiving but life-giving. In many respects, the resurrection of Christ corresponds to the Tree of Life, because it is how believers will move from mortality to immortality (1 Corinthians 15:53). Christ is the firstfruit of this movement or final transformation. As a result, Paul believes that Christ is the Second Adam who forges a new destiny for the human race, which is really the same destiny God has always had in mind. This destiny is to take humanity on a transforming journey in which they slowly come to share more and more of God's own life until, at last, they make the final leap to immortality.

In the Gospel of Luke, we learn that Jesus is the heir to David's throne, the One who will deliver His people from their sins and be a light unto the Gentiles (see Luke 1:35, 68-79; 2:29-32). The way Luke sees Jesus fulfilling His mission to deliver and restore is through the Holy Spirit. The angel Gabriel tells Mary that the Spirit will come upon her to conceive the child in her womb (1:35). Later, when Jesus enters the synagogue, He reads, "The Spirit of the Lord is upon Me, because He has anointed Me to preach the gospel to the poor; He has sent Me to heal the brokenhearted, to proclaim liberty to the captives" (4:18, *NKJV*).

The same Spirit who conceived Christ in Mary's womb anoints Him to bring liberty to those who are held captive in sin. For Luke, Christ is the true king who will bring about a new people of God, no longer bound by sin. Christ accomplishes this mission through the Spirit's work in His life.

Although the New Testament writers use different ideas to describe the work of Christ, they all agree that Christ is in the business of constructing a new race of people. In Christ, God is re-creating humanity so they can reach their complete potential as those created in God's image. In addition, the Gospel of Luke tells us that Christ constructed this new people of God through the Spirit. The Spirit conceived Christ in Mary and helped Him complete His mission. In a sense, the Spirit's conceiving Christ in Mary's womb and anointing Him for ministry corresponds to the two callings we have. We are reborn by the Spirit as those on the path of healing and gradually being transformed into this new humanity. Likewise, we are those anointed by the Spirit to extend God's invitation to the entire world to be part of this new humanity.

When we examine the relationship between the Spirit and Christ, we discover that the Spirit enables believers to live out their twin callings to reach their complete potential in and through Christ, and to be ambassadors of Christ. The Spirit is the key to understanding the connection between the calling to fellowship and the calling to witness.

In the previous chapter, I examined the nature of our adoption in Christ by looking at Galatians 4:4, 5, which indicates that God *sent* His Son and the Spirit of His Son to bring about our adoption. If we read the passage in light of Galatians 2:19, 20, where Paul declares "I have been crucified with Christ; and it is no longer I who live, but it is Christ who lives in me," we can see how Christ lives in a person. The Spirit makes Christ present. Moreover, Paul suggests that the Spirit helps the individual put on or be clothed with Christ. The Spirit joins us to Christ in order to reconstruct Christ's own life in us. The new humanity that Christ creates comes about as the Spirit unites us to Christ. To become a member of God's family is to become a member of this new humanity.

The life of discipleship is a life in the Spirit, because it is the Spirit who reproduces Christ's life, death and resurrection in us. While Christ remakes humanity and leads them on a new exodus out of sin and death so that they can reach their complete potential, the Spirit actualizes that exodus in the lives of believers as well as in the church, the new community God is creating.

Through the Spirit, we learn what it means to be created in the image of God. In the same way that the Spirit reproduces Christ's life in us, the Spirit distributes Christ's gifts to us. By distributing these gifts, the Spirit is anointing us to be ambassadors who proclaim God's message of salvation to the entire world. This is the calling to bear witness to what God is doing in Christ and in us. The Spirit helps us to fulfill both the calling to fellowship and the calling to witness because the Spirit connects us to Christ and makes us disciples.

THE CHURCH AND OUR TWIN VOCATIONS

If discipleship helps us to see *how* we live out our twin callings, then the church helps us discover *where* we do so. The church is the community of Christ's disciples. It is difficult to discuss the calling of God to discipleship without reference to the people of God. Although some Christians may want to live an isolated Christian life, cut off from their fellow believers, this is not what true Christianity is all about. Followers of Christ must participate in the body of Christ. There is no solitary existence for the Christian. Instead, there is only, as Ray Stedman put it, "body life."[11]

God calls all Christians to body life because His salvific work primarily involves establishing a new community who will be His people. There is little distinction between putting on Christ and belonging to the new community Christ has established. God does not "call" Christians to be part of the church as though they can live their Christian walk apart from it. To be a Christian is to be part of the church.

When speaking of Paul's view of salvation, Gordon Fee is as forceful as he can be: "Salvation is *never thought of simply as a one-on-one relationship with God*. While such a relationship is included, to be sure, to be saved means especially to be joined to the people of God" (emphasis mine).[12]

The focus of salvation in the New Testament is not on the individual as much as the creation of a people. Various phrases describe this new people: the household of God (Ephesians 2:19); the citizens of heaven (Ephesians 2:19; Philippians 3:20); the church (Acts 8:1, Revelation 2—3); the temple of the Spirit, with Christ as the chief cornerstone (Ephesians 2:20, 21; 1 Peter 2:4-8); the body of Christ (Romans 12:5) and the royal priesthood (1 Peter 2:9, 10). If we look for a Biblical passage that offers a direct command to belong to a local church, we are missing the point. The New Testament simply assumes that each believer is united to the body and participates in body life. Community life is at the heart of Christianity because God wants a people who reflect His own triune life. We are designed to be in relationship with God *and* with one another.

Water baptism and the Lord's Supper exemplify how this is the case. Both are *public* events, performed before and with one's fellow Christians. When believers are baptized, they are declaring to all present that they are followers of Christ, and that they belong to Christ's body.

Water baptism signals the believer's commitment to be part of God's new community and the local congregation's commitment to embrace the new believer. Baptism implies a covenant between fellow believers to be there for one another and help one another. It is a public declaration that the story of our lives as individuals will now become part of the collective story of the congregation before whom we were baptized. Our lives become strands of rope intertwined with all other believers who are members of our local congregation. As the public testimony of the Spirit's work to make us members of the body of Christ, water baptism compels us to view ourselves as part of this new community.

The same is true with the Lord's Supper. While many Christians view the practice of the Lord's Supper as simply a time to remember what Christ did on the Cross, we must think of it differently. This is not to deny that the Lord's Supper is a memorial of what Christ has done. However, that fact should not cloud its significance as a community event. Paul's description of the Lord's Supper in 1 Corinthians indicates that it occurred within the context of the church gathered together to share a meal. The problem with the Corinthians' practice of the Lord's Supper was they were engaged in backbiting. The divisions seemed to occur along economic lines, with the wealthy separating themselves from the poorer members of the congregation. The wealthy members denied the point of the Lord's Supper—"We who are many are one body, for we all partake of the one bread" (10:17). To abuse the body of Christ by introducing division is equivalent to abusing Christ, which is why Paul says that some were eating and drinking judgment upon themselves (11:29-33).[13]

Christ is building a new community of people who truly reflect God's life by living together in peace. The Lord's Supper is the public event that announces that unity. We are one body because we eat one bread. When we participate in the Lord's Supper, we publicly commit ourselves to be part of Christ's body. It is a renewal of our covenant with God to be His people and with one another to live as His people in unity and peace.

The calling to fellowship with God and to witness for Him must be lived out through this new community He is forming. If the call to fellowship is a call to realize our complete potentials as those created in the image of God, we cannot neglect membership in the *new humanity* Christ is forming. We bring about God's call to be human beings in the new humanity. The church is where we learn how to put on Christ by growing and maturing in that relationship. By "the church," I do not mean the physical building, but the community—the group of people who identify themselves as disciples of Christ. Too often, we say, "Let's go to church," as if we are driving to a building to hear a speech, sing some songs and then go home. When we go to church, we are gathering as a community of disciples. We learn how to put on Christ and realize our potential in and through a community of believers who pray for us, challenge us and push us, in short, who live and die with us. This is what it means to intertwine the story of one's life with others. We become transformed so that we reflect God's life by learning how to live together as the community of God.

How do we know what it means to bear one another's burdens if we don't belong to a community where we practice it? How can we sympathize with the problems others face when we never take the time to learn about those problems and pray for them? Praying for the sick and downtrodden is a transforming act that teaches us to care for others as Christ cares for them and live as we were designed to live—in relationship with God and with one another.

I learned what it meant to love people through the difficult periods of my adolescence by watching others in my local church and observing how they responded to one another. As we shared meals, wept with one another, rejoiced over one another's triumphs and experienced life together, we were transformed by God's grace. We learned what it meant to be human in relationship with one another as we learned what it meant to be the new humanity that God called into existence.

The importance of belonging to the body of Christ is that we are incorporated into a community of disciples who are putting on Christ by learning to love and care for one another "in the power of the Spirit." We should not lose sight of the fact that Paul's letters are addressed to local churches. When Paul says to the church at Ephesus, "Be imitators of God as dear children. And walk in love, as Christ also has loved us" (Ephesians 5:1, 2, *NKJV*), he is not talking about an attitude Christians should have in general. There is not an expectation that the Ephesians will learn to love people in the Roman world whom they have not met. Rather, he is telling the Christians who are gathered together in Ephesus as a community that they should love one another. When he tells the church at Rome that the strong should support the weak among them (Romans 15:1), he is referring to the local churches in that city. Paul is essentially saying to them, "When you assemble together as a community, the strong among you should help the weak." Believers cannot fulfill the call to change and put on Christ unless they learn to care for one another. Only when we are face to face with the real-life problems of our fellow Christians do we begin to learn what it means to love and to embrace. And, when we learn to love, we are transformed.

The church is the place where discipleship is lived out. We become truly human when we learn to live with other humans and walk with them through life. Walking by the Spirit is a way of living that the requires the community of faith, which is why Paul follows his admonition to the Galatians with the advice to "bear one another's burdens" (6:2). This means that our churches should facilitate body life. Admittedly, it is easier for smaller and medium-sized churches to promote body life than larger churches, but this does not mean that larger churches cannot promote community. Small groups are one way larger churches have succeeded in reconnecting their members to one another. In the end though, each church must become intentional about promoting an environment where church members become responsible for one another in tangible ways. It is not enough simply to pray for a request spoken from a pulpit. As believers invest in one another's lives, they learn to be true disciples of Christ. Like the early church, modern-day churches must seek to continue in apostles' fellowship, in the breaking of bread and in prayers (Acts 2:42).

When the church becomes a community of disciples, where each person invests in the life of that community, it becomes the place where the call to witness occurs. God's call to witness involves a recognition on the part of the community that God is working in a particular way in the life of one person. How can any community say that God works in an individual's life when their lives are not intertwined with the life of that person? The New Testament suggests that the calling to witness normally comes in the midst of community life. Paul (Saul) and Barnabas were set apart for missionary work to the Gentiles as the church was gathered together for worship (13:1-3). After the Spirit identified Paul and Barnabas, the church "laid their hands on them" to commission them for the task (v. 3).

Years later, when Paul described Timothy's call, he used the same language, telling Timothy not to neglect the gift in him, "which was given to you by prophecy with the laying on of hands of the eldership" (1 Timothy 4:14, *NKJV*). In both cases, the community of disciples recognized God's gifts in particular individuals and sent those individuals forth to do the work of the ministry.

We should not lose sight of the fact that commissioning comes through the laying on of hands. The symbol of human touch is powerful. In extending His blessing through human touch, God is actively seeking to promote community life by strengthening relationships among His people. When we become channels of God's grace to other people, God is forging a relational link that we cannot overlook. At minimum, this should tell us that human relationships are important to God. In the touch of one person by another, God breaks down dividing walls of hostility like gender and race and shows us that His kingdom will consist of people from every tribe and tongue. Although God can work apart from humans, He calls us to lay hands on one another because He not only wants to connect us to Himself, but also to one another. The calling to fellowship and the calling to witness are bound up with one another. Even the act of commissioning a person to be a witness for the Kingdom helps promote fellowship with God and fellow believers.

SUMMARY

The call to be human is God's general call to the entire race to be all He has designed us to be. It is a call to realize our complete potential in and through fellowship with God. God has made us for Himself.

In calling us to relationship with Himself, He also calls us to be in relationship with one another. The image of God is best seen in the relationships that exist between human beings. Community life, in all of its dimensions—family life or church life—remains bound up in the call to be human.

Although sin warps our relationships and becomes an insurmountable obstacle to realizing our full potential, God redeems a new humanity from sin and death through Christ and the Spirit. We are called to be part of this new humanity, the church, because it is where we live out our discipleship. The church is the place where we learn what it means to love and to be human. It is also the place where we receive our commissioning to be God's ambassadors, proclaiming His divine call to fellowship to the entire world. Here is where God's twin calls come full circle. The call to witness complements the call to fellowship. We are witnessing to the work God is doing in us and in the community to which we belong. By means of the gifts the Spirit imparts and the life the Spirit brings, we proclaim that God is calling us to participate in His life and to share that life with others. This is the good work that God in Christ Jesus has prepared in advance for us to do (Ephesians 2:10).

ENDNOTES

[1] I take the phrases "calling of fellowship" and "calling of witness" from George Hunsinger. See his *How to Read Karl Barth: The Shape of His Theology* (New York: Oxford UP, 1991) 173-183.

[2] Augustine, *Confessions*, Book 1, ch. 1. Loeb Classical Library (Cambridge, MA: Harvard UP, 1912).

[3] *Tanakh: The Holy Scriptures, The New JPS Translation According to the Traditional Hebrew Text* (Philadelphia: Jewish Publication Society, 1988).

[4] See H.W. Wolff, *Anthropology of the Old Testament*, trans. Margaret Kohl (Philadelphia: Fortress, 1974) 159.

[5] Wolff, 160. See also C. Westermann, *Genesis 1-11: A Commentary*, trans. John J. Scullion (Minneapolis: Augsburg Fortress, 1984) 157, 158.

[6] Wolff, 157.

[7] *Tanakh.*

[8] *Church of God Declaration of Faith* in *Our Statements of Faith* (Cleveland, TN: Pathway, n.d.) 4.

[9] See Harold W. Attridge, *Hebrews*: *Hermeneia* (Philadelphia: Fortress, 1989) 356.

[10] John Ziesler, *Pauline Christianity*, rev. ed. (Oxford: Oxford UP, 1990) 53.

[11] Ray Stedman, *Body Life* (Glendale, CA: Regal, 1972).

[12] Gordon Fee, *God's Empowering Presence* (Peabody, MA: Hendrichson, 1994) 846.

[13] Gordon Fee, *The First Epistle to the Corinthians*, New International Commentary on the New Testament (Grand Rapids: Eerdmans, 1987) 533, 534.

CHAPTER 5

Eternal Election

Blessed be the God and Father of our Lord Jesus Christ, who has blessed us in Christ with every spiritual blessing in the heavenly places, just as he chose us in Christ before the foundation of the world to be holy and blameless before him in love (Ephesians 1:3, 4).

When I first became a Christian, I wanted to study the Bible as much as possible. Like many young Christians, I was curious to discover the answers to numerous questions about Christianity. I had conversations with my Catholic friends about the differences in what we believed, argued with my Baptist friends over whether Christians were eternally secure, and debated with many of my non-Pentecostal friends about the baptism in the Holy Spirit and other issues. Looking back, these debates and conversations were fairly light, although at the time, I thought I was engaging in deep theological discourse about the biggest questions of life.

One line of questioning that emerged was the relationship between divine election, predestination and free choice. Soon after I began college, I learned how long the issue had been debated by Christians. For Protestants, this debate goes back as far as the origins of Protestantism and came to a head at the beginning of the 1600s, when the followers of James Arminius proposed an alternate explanation to the one given by John Calvin. Calvin had suggested that God actively predestines some to hell and others to heaven—the doctrine known as double predestination. Although Arminius studied in the college Calvin had founded, he rejected Calvin's interpretation. Arminius believed that double predestination could not be true, given the Scriptural evidence of God as perfectly good and perfectly loving. Instead, he sought to work out a system of predestination that centered around the idea of the corporate body of Christ. As a result of Arminius' disagreement with Calvin's position, a debate broke out (Calvinism vs. Arminianism) that continues to the present day.

While some may consider the debate over predestination and God's eternal election as puzzling and mostly irrelevant, our views on predestination are important for two reasons. First, what we believe to a large degree determines how we behave, and that includes what we believe about predestination.

Second, our views about predestination inform what we think about God and the way God works in the world, especially in His affairs with humans. The doctrine of predestination relates to God's providence, or how He governs and cares for the Creation. If you think God demonstrates His care by predetermining the eternal destinies of humans, then that belief will affect the way you pray and pursue a holy life. Conversely, if you think God allows humans the freedom to determine their own destinies, then that will also affect how you pray, engage in evangelism and live a holy life.

In this chapter, I will discuss this complex issue with the intent of acting as a guide who is familiar with the terrain and point out some of the obstacles. My view is not the definitive answer to the question of predestination and eternal election, but I hope that it is *an* answer that will prove beneficial to those pursuing holiness. After working through the issue, the importance of the debate over predestination and its relationship to human freedom will become clear.

GETTING SOME IDEAS STRAIGHT

For the sake of clarity, a few points must be addressed before attempting to set forth a view on this topic. First, both election and predestination are Biblical concepts and cannot be avoided. The question is not *whether* I believe in predestination, but *what* I believe about predestination. Paul declares, "For those whom he foreknew he also predestined to be conformed to the image of his Son" (Romans 8:29), and spends Romans 9—11 explaining what he means by that statement.

In the Book of Ephesians, the idea of being "destined" or "predestined" occurs several times throughout the first chapter (Ephesians 1:4, 5, 11). One could even interpret Jesus' statement that "no one can come to me unless it is granted by the Father" (John 6:65) as implying eternal predestination. Although it may be necessary to reject certain views of predestination and election, this is different from rejecting them altogether.

Once we see predestination and election as Biblical concepts, we need to know what these specific terms mean. *Election* is a noun from which we get the verb "to elect." Both the noun and the verb have to do with choice. In the same way that an individual makes a choice during a political election, when we speak of eternal election we are talking about God's choice. If understood correctly, the term *predestination* further clarifies God's choice by indicating when that choice occurred.

Predestination refers to what God determines (chooses) to do, and in fact does, beforehand. In this sense, it is synonymous with the term *foreordain*. When we put both terms together, they refer to God choosing a plan of action and implementing it prior to choices made by others. In fact, God makes choices in much the same way that we do. God plans ahead or predetermines what He is going to do just as we plan our day ahead of time. Once God formulates a plan of action, He carries it out. Thinking about predestination and election as indicating God's plan of action for the universe, including humanity, can help us sort through the issues that arise.

Since both election and predestination refer to God's prior choices, they refer primarily to God's will and not God's knowledge. The difference between God's will and God's knowledge is equal to the difference between what God does and what God knows. While this distinction may seem minor, it is important. For example, if God has perfect knowledge of the future, then He already knows who will and will not go to heaven. The fact that God possesses this kind of knowledge does not mean He wills to send some to heaven and others to hell. To say God *predestines* is to say that He *wills* beforehand that something will happen, not that He *knows* beforehand what will happen.

Most Christians believe that God knows the future. Our prayers seem to depend on this fact. This is why we trust God to guide us. Consequently, God can know the future perfectly and not determine by His will what will happen. God can *know* whether the president of the United States will be assassinated in 2050 and not *predetermine* that the president be assassinated.

God's knowledge of the future does not mean that God causes or wills it to happen. Election and predestination both refer to what God wills to do, or the implementation of His plan of action for the universe. With these distinctions in mind, I want to examine predestination and election from three perspectives: electing a people, electing a person and electing a plan.

ELECTING A PEOPLE

Chosen People in the Old Testament. The place to begin a discussion of predestination and election is with God's choice of Israel as His people. In the Old Testament, election has more to do with God choosing a group of people than specific individuals. The focus of election always centers on the community or the people of Israel. When the Old Testament refers to God's choice of an individual, it is because the person represents or forms part of this larger group. For example, the story of Abraham's unconditional election by God is really the story of Israel's election (Genesis 12:1-3; 18:18; 22:18). Abraham's story is another way of God saying to Israel, "You are My special treasure above all other nations" (see Exodus 19:5; Deuteronomy 7:6-8).

This story is not about Abraham's secret election before the world began. Instead, the focus on Abraham has to do with the group. One could say that the Old Testament describes the election of Israel as the people of God by telling the story of how God worked in the life of Israel's ancestor, Abraham. This is why God announces Himself as the God of Abraham, Isaac and Jacob all through the Old Testament. It is God's way of identifying Israel as His people.

A second example is the famous text of Malachi 1:2, 3, where God says, "Jacob I have loved; but Esau I have hated" (*NKJV*). Jacob represents Israel and Esau represents Edom, a nation that became Israel's enemy (see Numbers 20:14-20). There is no indication that God chooses the individual Jacob and rejects Esau from all eternity. Instead, this is another way of describing His choice of the nation of Israel. God reminds Israel that it is the object of His love, not Edom.

Malachi also indicates that not all Israel will be accepted by God. Even though God loves the nation of Israel, individual Israelites may be rejected if they do not straighten up. The problem is that some Israelites fail to worship God properly (1:7, 12), others fail to abstain from marrying foreign wives (2:11), and still others continue to rob God of tithes and offerings (3:8). When Malachi separates the righteous from the wicked, he has in mind two distinct groups of Israelites.[1] The righteous Israelites are those who fear God, listen to Him and meditate on His name, while the wicked are proud who tempt God by their failure to adhere to His covenant.

The Book of Malachi begins with an affirmation of God's love for Israel as a group and then warns that certain individual Israelites may remove themselves from this group by their actions. Although Malachi 1:2, 3 may seem to refer to the individual election of Jacob and Esau, it is another way of focusing on the nation or the community.

Although the Old Testament concept of election refers to God's choice of a group, it also indicates the open-ended membership of this elected group. That is, those who belong to the elect remain up for grabs. Indeed, the prophetic books provide hints that God will extend His election beyond the borders of national Israel. Nowhere is this idea more clearly stated than in Isaiah 19, where Isaiah describes the conversion of Egypt and Assyria. Isaiah declares, "On that day Israel will be the third with Egypt and Assyria, a blessing in the midst of the earth, whom the Lord of hosts has blessed, saying, 'Blessed be Egypt *my* people, and

Assyria the work of *my* hands, and Israel *my* heritage'"
(vv. 24, 25, emphasis mine). According to Isaiah, the
chosen people of God now include Israel's neighbors
to the north and the south. Israel still occupies a central place as "a blessing in the midst of the earth (v. 24),
but the chosen people no longer include the physical
descendants of Abraham only.[2]

The story of Jonah further attests to an extension of
God's chosen people beyond the borders of Israel. The
Book of Jonah opens with God's command that Jonah
go to Nineveh, a city in the Assyrian empire, and deliver a message of judgment and salvation. As Douglas
Stuart suggests, the central point of the book is to challenge Jonah's national pride by asserting God's freedom to show compassion on anyone.[3] God asks Jonah,
"Is it right for you to be angry?" (4:4, 9).

Jonah is clearly upset when God extends forgiveness
and mercy instead of judgment to the Assyrians. Jonah
even cites his anger as the reason why he ran away from
God. God's final response to Jonah is to ask, "Should I
not be concerned about Nineveh?" (v. 11). Just because
Israel is God's chosen nation, Jonah should not make
the mistake of thinking God cannot and will not invite
others to follow Him and be part of His people.

Another dimension in the election of Israel is the
fluctuating number of the chosen people. God does
not set in stone an exact number of His elect people. We
can see this idea expressed most clearly in the concept
of a remnant. When Elijah despairs that all Israel has
forsaken the covenant, God comforts him by appealing

to a remnant of those in Israel who have not bowed their knee to the false god, Baal (1 Kings 19:18).[4]

Not all Israelites are faithful. This much should be clear from Malachi's message. Although God chose the nation of Israel, many Israelites continue to be unfaithful to the covenant. In light of this problem, it becomes increasingly difficult to identify who does and does not belong to the people of God. While Israel as a whole remains the chosen people of God, individual Israelites move in and out of the group. The idea of a remnant identifies a group within the nation of Israel who had remained faithful. There is always a recognition in the Old Testament that Israelites who were unfaithful ceased to be part of the chosen people of God.[5] As a result, it is never clear who exactly belongs to the elected nation of Israelites. The number keeps shifting in light of the unfaithfulness of individual Israelites.

We can see this continuous shift by looking closely at God's choice of Jeroboam to lead the northern kingdom of Israel (1 Kings 11). Although Solomon is David's heir, toward the end of his reign he displays the same kind of unfaithfulness as some of the other Israelites. Because of Solomon's unfaithfulness, God rips the kingdom from the hands of his son and extends His choice to Jeroboam as the one through whom a new kingly dynasty would be formed. God tells Jeroboam, "I will be with you, and will build you an enduring house, as I built for David" (v. 38).

This is powerful language. There is no doubt that

God is placing His blessing on Jeroboam, even promising that Jeroboam's descendants will remain on the throne forever (an *enduring* house). However, Jeroboam's own faithful response must follow God's choice. When Jeroboam becomes unfaithful, God withdraws His promise (14:6-13). The fascinating part of this story is how quickly God chooses and then rejects Jeroboam. Nevertheless, the northern kingdom of Israel remains intact, because God's rejection of Jeroboam in no way implies that God has rejected Israel as His chosen people. The group remains, while individuals come and go.

We can now draw some conclusions about the concept of election in the Old Testament. Election primarily concerns a group of people, and even God's choice of Abraham must be viewed in these terms. This means that election is corporate in nature, not individualistic. Think of a corporation like General Motors with lots of employees where individual employees come and go, but the corporation remains. Likewise, Old Testament writers were never able to define this elect group clearly. Its exact number remains open-ended and even other nations are invited to be a part of it.

Finally, the ultimate aim of Israel's election is to extend God's message of salvation to the entire world. We find this in God's promise to Abraham that "in you all the families of the earth shall be blessed" (Genesis 12:3). It is also present in the divine call for Israel to be a holy nation of priests (Exodus 19:6) so that she can proclaim God's message to the entire world.

Chosen People in Romans. As a result of this survey of election in the Old Testament, we are in a better position to understand Paul's view of election and predestination. Romans 9–11 is the place where the debate over predestination is fought. According to one defender of Calvinism, Romans 9 contains the "most significant passage in the New Testament" about predestination.[6] For that reason, we need to get a better grasp of Paul's concept of election in Romans. Throughout this brief discussion, we need to keep in mind the Old Testament concept of corporate election.

Before turning to Romans 9—11, it is important to understand how those chapters fit into Paul's argument in Romans 1—8. The following outline indicates the flow of Paul's thought and how Romans 9—11 represents the logical culmination of his argument. In brief, one could structure Romans 1—8 this way:[7]

1. Romans 1:1-17: The righteousness of God is revealed in the gospel of Jesus Christ. It is important to keep in mind that Paul thinks of the righteousness of God in terms of God's faithfulness to the covenant.

2. Romans 1:18—3:20: Both Jew and Gentile alike stand under sin because both groups prove to be unfaithful.

3. Romans 3:21—4:25: Salvation rests upon the faithfulness of Jesus Christ for all who believe in Him in the same way that Abraham believed in God.

4. Romans 5:1—6:23: God's faithfulness is demonstrated by the faithfulness of Jesus Christ in two ways: (a) Christ's faithful obedience versus

Adam's disobedience; (b) Christ's faithfulness in liberating from the "Egypt" of slavery to sin all those joined to Him.

5. Romans 7:1—8:39: The problem of unfaithfulness is not a problem of God's law but in the weakness of persons to fulfill it (7:1-25). The Spirit corrects the problem of the lack of faithfulness on the part of God's covenant people by enabling them to walk in light of the Law and so fulfill it (8:1-39).

This outline of Romans 1—8 suggests that God demonstrates His covenant faithfulness to the chosen people of God in and through Christ's death and resurrection and the Spirit's transforming power. This is the gospel, or good news, according to Paul. The power of God for salvation rests on God's faithfulness to liberate from the bondage of sin the Jew first, then also the Gentile through Christ and the Spirit (1:16). As the ultimate purpose of Romans 1—8, God's demonstration of His faithfulness in salvation sets up Paul's immediate expression of anguish in 9:1-5 with regard to his own people, the Jews.

If God demonstrates His faithfulness to the covenant with Israel by Christ and the Spirit, then why are so many individual Jews turning away? After all, Israel is the elect people of God and those through whom the promises of God flow (9:4-5). Where do the Jews fit in the plan of God? The issue surrounding the status of national Israel as the chosen people of God is the logical question that emerges in light of what Paul said in Romans 1—8. This issue becomes even more apparent given the fact that many Israelites rejected the gospel. One can see why Paul is in anguish over his own people. Moreover, the rejection of the gospel by many Israelites suggests that maybe God's Word has no effect. Can we claim that God remains faithful when so many Jewish people do not embrace Christ?

Romans 9—11 explores the issue of God's faithfulness and Jewish disobedience in light of the election of the nation of Israel. The nation of Israel *is* the chosen (elect) people of God and yet Israelites reject Christ, while numerous Gentiles accept Christ. Paul's answer to this dilemma is in line with the Old Testament concept of corporate election, in which God has an elect group of people, while individuals move in and out of the group. More specifically, Paul builds on the idea of a remnant of the faithful in order to argue that the chosen people never included all of Abraham's descendants.

Paul begins his argument, "For not all Israelites truly belong to Israel" (9:6). In other words, not all of Abraham's physical descendants belong to the elect people of God. This point explains why Luke Timothy Johnson forcefully states, "Paul's topic is not the eternal predestination of individual human souls to heaven or hell. . . . Here as throughout the letter, but even more explicitly, Paul conceives of salvation . . . as a matter of belonging to God's people."[8] To read Romans 9—11 as focusing upon God's electing individuals to heaven or hell is to miss the point of those chapters completely. Their entire purpose is to say that God continues to have a chosen people, a remnant, which includes faithful Jews and faithful Gentiles.

By examining Paul's argument more closely, the outline of his argument that not all of Abraham's physical descendants are part of God's elect people emerges. Following Malachi, Paul asserts that both the children of Jacob (the Israelites) and the children of Esau (the Edomites) were physical descendants of Abraham. However, the fact that both groups could claim to be descended from Abraham did not mean that both were part of God's elect body (cf. Romans 9:11-12).

It is important to remember that Jacob and Esau represent distinct groups of people, not individuals. The difference between Israel and Edom allows Paul to make a second point that even among the children of Jacob some are faithful and some are not. This is where Paul inserts the idea of a remnant—an idea he gets from the Old Testament prophets (cf. Romans 9:25-29). There remains a remnant of God's chosen people, which includes all those who were faithful to God. The first step in Paul's argument is to establish that God has a chosen people and that this chosen people never included all Israelites.

The second step in the argument draws upon the Old Testament idea that God opens up His elect body to include the Gentiles. God actively seeks to extend the boundaries of His elect people beyond national identity, a point the Old Testament prophets had already made. For Paul, the way God extends those boundaries is through Christ and the Spirit. This is the new work God is doing. How individuals, Jews and Gentiles, join themselves to this new work of God remains the same: faith. In Romans 9:30—10:15, Paul makes clear one point: "If you confess with your mouth the Lord Jesus and believe in your heart that God has raised Him from the dead, you will be saved" (10:9, *NKJV*). God's remnant, the elect group of people, includes both Jews and Gentiles who express faith in Christ. It is a corporate body open to all who believe.

Some suggest that a corporate concept of election necessarily includes individuals. As such, God must predetermine the destiny of individuals to predetermine the destiny of a group. This conclusion can only be reached if one ignores how Paul brings his discussion of God's chosen people to a close in Romans 11.

Paul uses an agricultural illustration to reinforce his understanding of how individuals become part of the chosen people of God (vv. 16-24). The illustration centers on an olive tree with different branches. The tree itself, which Paul also refers to as the root (9:18), represents the nation of Israel, the chosen people of God. He divides the branches into two types, natural branches and wild branches. The natural branches refer to Israelites and the wild branches refer to Gentile Christians. Paul then clearly indicates that Gentiles (the wild branches) who accept Christ are grafted onto the people of God (the tree) even while Jews (the natural branches) who reject Christ are cut off.

However, just as quickly, he suggests that Gentiles who are grafted onto the people of God could also be cut off. Consequently, Paul maintains the idea that God has chosen a group of people while also stressing that individuals move in and out of this chosen group. There is no secret predestination of one person to heaven or another person to hell. If one were to ask Paul how someone becomes part of the people of God, he would state, "Because of unbelief they [the natural branches] were broken off, and you [the wild branches] stand by faith" (11:20, *NKJV*).

God's eternal choice does not rest upon individual persons, but on a group of people. Indeed, it seems perfectly acceptable to say that part of what God predetermines is that He will have a people for Himself. Scripture uses the terms *election, chosen people, remnant,* and so forth, to refer to this group. Even in Paul's writings, God's choice always seems to center on a group of people. However, the New Testament does include within the concept of corporate election the eternal choice of an individual person. Moreover, the chosen people of God are defined exclusively in terms of God's election of this one person—Jesus Christ.

ELECTING A PERSON

One of the differences between election in the Old Testament and the New Testament is that the New Testament views Christ as the foundation of election. What this suggests is that the person of Christ becomes the focus of God's eternal choice. God predetermines that Christ will be the One through whom the world will be reconciled. Consequently, God's chosen people are defined by their connection to God's chosen Messiah.

But this is not all. If we understand *who* Christ is, we can detect another side to His election. Christ not only is fully human, He also is fully divine. He is both the human being who is chosen by God and the God who chooses, wrapped up in one. To see Christ as the foundation of our election, we must consider the fact that He defines God's elect people by revealing Himself as the God who elects and the human who is elected.

The idea that Christ is both the God who chooses and the human being who is chosen comes from a Swiss German theologian, Karl Barth.[9] In his approach to predestination, Barth focuses on how the New Testament centers election on Christ, especially in light of the fact that Christ is fully God and fully man.

When we view Christ as fully God, we are focusing on His complete equality with the Father and His absolute divinity. Christ is the eternal Word of God who was with God in the beginning (John 1:1) and who is the exact representation of "God's very being" (Hebrews 1:3). As the eternal Word of God, Christ shares in God's decision to elect.

By viewing Christ as fully human, we are recognizing His complete equality with all humans. Christ is Jesus of Nazareth, the human being who lived, died on a cross and was raised from the dead.

Like two sides of the same coin, Christ's divinity and humanity are the two aspects of His identity we must keep before us. Unless Christ is fully divine, we have no guarantee that God is establishing true fellowship with us; unless Christ is fully human, we have no guarantee that we have true fellowship with God.

In the Incarnation, God builds a bridge of salvation between humanity and Divinity. The Incarnation is nothing less than the eternal Son of God, the second person of the Trinity, becoming a human being. The very word *incarnation* means to be in-fleshed or to take on flesh.

Barth believes that one can see God's eternal election in the decision of the Son of God to become a human. If the eternal Son is truly God, then God's decision to choose must be made by the Son, as well as the Father and the Spirit. It is a decision made by the triune God, who is Father, Son and Holy Spirit. What is that decision? Is it a secret decision to save some and reject others? Barth's answer is an emphatic "No!" As he states, "The eternal will of God in the election of Jesus Christ is His will to give Himself for the sake of man as created by Him and fallen from Him. According to the Bible this was what took place in the incarnation of the Son of God, in His death and passion, in His resurrection from the dead. We must think of this as the content of the eternal divine predestination."[10]

God's eternal choice is nothing less than to give His own life for others by becoming Jesus of Nazareth. "For God so loved the world that He gave His only begotten Son" (John 3:16, *NKJV*). Examining election from the perspective of Christ reveals that divine election is the Son of God's eternal choice to build a bridge by taking on flesh.

If God's decision is to become a human being, who is the one elected? The answer is simple: the human being the Son of God became. While the Old Testament sees Israel as the one chosen to be the elect people of God, the New Testament suggests that Christ is the One chosen. In choosing to become a human being, the eternal Son of God was choosing to save the world.

Notice how 1 Peter 1:20 puts it: "He was destined before the foundation of the world, but was revealed at the end of the ages for your sake." In this statement, Peter places the coming of Christ firmly in God's eternal election.[11] It was part of God's plan from the very beginning to choose the world through Jesus Christ. Peter describes the human side of God's choice. The eternal Son of God chose to become a particular human being, Jesus of Nazareth. In making this eternal choice, God was choosing to save the world through the one Christ, who is the only One suitable to build the bridge because He is fully divine and fully human.

There is an important practical point to Barth's emphasis on Christ. We can be assured that God's election extends to us because of Christ. For Barth, there is no secret will of God predetermining who will go to heaven and who will not go to heaven because God makes His will known in Christ. To put it another way, Christ *is* the God who chooses, so if you want to know God's will, you need only look at Christ.

Secondly, we don't need to worry about *who* gets chosen by God because we know that Christ is the one chosen. Again, there is no secret number God has

selected from among the peoples of the earth. God has
selected Christ. He is the one individual whose destiny
God has determined.

Barth insisted that in and through Christ we can see
God's divine "Yes" to humanity.[12] When the eternal
Son of God *chose* to take on human flesh and become
a man, He was saying, "I choose humanity in this one
man, Jesus of Nazareth." This is the divine *yes*. As Paul
puts it, "For the Son of God, Jesus Christ, whom we
proclaimed among you . . . was not 'Yes and No'; but
in him it is always 'Yes.' For *in him* every one of God's
promises is a 'Yes' " (2 Corinthians 1:19- 20, emphasis mine). God's promises become available to humanity because the election of God moves from Christ as
God to Christ as man to us.

**God's Election to Build a Bridge Through the
Person of Christ**
From Christ as God → to Christ as man →
to all those "in Christ"
(His elect body)

The eternal Son of God, the second person of the
Trinity, chose to become a human being, so that in the
eternal election to be Jesus of Nazareth He might save
the whole world. Far from being a dark decision, God's
eternal election ought to give us the complete assurance
and comfort that God is always working for us, not
against us.

As the One chosen by God to restore fellowship with
humanity, Christ now defines the chosen people of

God. By saying that Christ *defines* the chosen people of God, I simply mean we can *identify* who the elect are in reference to Christ. I can identify myself as part of the elect because I belong to Christ and Christ belongs to me. The New Testament describes this connection to Christ primarily in terms of being united to Christ.

Throughout Paul's letters, we find numerous references to being "in Christ," "in Him," "in whom" and "in Christ Jesus," all of which point toward our union with Christ. We can see the connection between election and Christ most clearly in Ephesians where Paul declares that believers have been chosen *in Christ* before the foundation of the world (1:4).

John uses the terms "abiding" and "remaining" to describe the union between Christ and believers. This is especially the case in John 15 where Jesus describes Himself as the true vine and believers as the branches. As one commentator suggests, "Jesus redefines the elect as those who abide in him." [13] Even in 1 Peter, we find the idea that God "has called you to his eternal glory *in Christ*" (5:10, emphasis mine). In all of these passages, individuals become part of God's elect as they become united to Christ and form part of His body.

Now that we have examined the role of Christ, I hope that it is becoming clear how God's election of a people and God's election of a person work together. God has chosen in eternity that He will have a people. This much should be clear from our examination of the Old Testament and Romans. However, God has also predestined Christ to be the One who will save the world. All those who become united to Christ share or participate in God's election of Christ. He is the vine and believers are the branches grafted on to His life, death and resurrection. Once grafted on to Christ, we become the corporate body of Christ, the chosen ones from every tribe, nation and tongue. Election is still corporate, but the corporation is defined by Christ and not by national Israel. All of this leads us to the final part of God's eternal election: His plan.

ELECTING A PLAN

God's election of a people and a person naturally tells us that God has always had a plan. The plan concerns how individuals become part of God's chosen people. This is the third element in divine election. In choosing Christ to be the One slain from the foundation of the world, God also chooses the means of salvation, or the way individuals will bring about their salvation. Given the previous discussion, I need only point out two essential components to this plan.

First, God decides that Christ will be the way of salvation. Second, God also eternally wills that all those who express faith in Christ will be saved or become part of God's chosen people. Both of these components represent God's election of a people and a person with faith as the means to lay hold of Christ. So God not only predestines that Christ be the way, the truth and the life, and that all those who are "in Christ" will be His elect, but He also predestines faith as the way to unlock the benefits of Christ's life, death and resurrection.

What God Predestines

A People

God will have a chosen people (corporate election).

A Person

Christ, as God, chooses to create a people when He becomes a human being who dies for the whole world.

A Plan

The chosen people of God are all those who believe on the Lord Jesus Christ and are united to Him.

SUMMARY

God invites the entire world to become part of the body of Christ. He does not single out one group of people over another as the special recipients of His election. The divine choice from all eternity is that God will have a chosen people who come into existence as they embrace Christ, the chosen One of God by faith. Moreover, as we have seen, the doctrine of election is God's divine "Yes" to humanity.

Rather than working against the pursuit of holiness, we should see election and predestination as giving us the comfort we need to pursue holiness. Why? Because election tells us that God has already built the bridge between humanity and divinity in Christ. Before we existed, God was working all things together for our ultimate good by deciding that He himself would seek us out to transform us into His likeness, to heal our disease and to restore fellowship with Him.

God exercises His providence, or care, for His creation by joining Himself to it in and through Christ and taking its sorrows upon Himself. "He was wounded for our transgressions, He was bruised for our iniquities; the chastisement for our peace (*shalom*) was upon Him, and by His stripes we are healed" (Isaiah 53:5, *NKJV*). Suffering gives way to a kind of healing that produces wholeness and reconciliation in that the chastisement of God's servant brought *shalom*.[14]

Election tells us that the transformation from one diseased by sin to one healed and made holy concerns our becoming the image of Christ, who Himself is the image of the invisible God (Colossians 1:15). Finally, it tells us firmly that our restoration of fellowship is a cooperative affair with God. In and through the God-man, Jesus Christ, God has predetermined to enter into a partnership with humanity in order to bring about our salvation.

ENDNOTES

[1] See Jon L. Berquist, *Judaism in Persia's Shadow: A Social and Historical Approach* (Minneapolis: Fortress, 1995) 100, 101. Berquist suggests that Malachi identifies an "in-group" of Israelites who are faithful and a rejected "out-group" who are not faithful.

[2] Joseph Blenkinsopp, Isaiah 1—39, *The Anchor Bible*, vol.19 (New York: Doubleday, 2000) 319, 320.

[3] Douglas Stuart, *Hosea—Jonah, Word Biblical Commentary vol. 31* (Waco, TX: Word, 1987) 435.

[4] For further examination of the concept of remnant, see H.H. Rowley, *The Biblical Doctrine of Election* (London: Lutterworth, 1950) 69-94.

[5] Rowley, 69.

[6] R.C. Sproul, *Chosen by God* (Wheaton, IL: Tyndale, 1986) 148.

[7] My summary of Romans 1—8 represents a composite picture I have drawn from the work of Gordon Fee, N.T. Wright and Luke Timothy Johnson. See Fee, *God's Empowering Presence*, 472-476; Johnson, *Reading Romans*, viiff; Wright, "New Exodus, New Inheritance: The Narrative Substructure of Romans 3—8," *Romans and the People of God: Essays in Honor of Gordon D. Fee*, eds. S.K. Soderlund and N.T. Wright (Grand Rapids: Eerdmans, 1999) 26-35.

[8] Luke Timothy Johnson, *Reading Romans* (New York: Crossroad, 1997) 140.

[9] See Karl Barth, *Church Dogmatics*, vol. 2, part 2, eds. G.W. Bromiley and T.F. Torrance (Edinburgh: T & T Clark, 1957).

[10] Barth, 161.

[11] See I. Howard Marshall, *1 Peter*, *The IVP New Testament Commentary Series*, ed. G.R. Osborne (Downers Grove, IL: InterVarsity, 1991) 55-57; and Andrew Chester and Ralph P. Martin, *The Theology of the Letters of James, Peter, and Jude* (Cambridge: Cambridge UP, 1994) 108, 109.

[12] Barth, 169ff.

[13] See Larry W. Hurtado, *Lord Jesus Christ: Devotion to Jesus in Earliest Christianity* (Grand Rapids: Eerdmans, 2003) 373.

[14] See J. Blenkinsopp, *Isaiah 40-55*, The Anchor Bible (New York: Doubleday, 2000) 352, 353.

CHAPTER 6

Divine Grace and Human Cooperation

For this I toil and struggle with all the energy that he powerfully inspires within me (Colossians 1:29).

One of the main purposes for the doctrine of eternal election is to show that salvation remains a work of God's free grace. Election indicates that God was working to bring us to salvation long before we decided to embrace Christ. The fact that God works first and all our work is merely a response to His prior initiatives tells us that we are saved by grace, not of ourselves, "lest anyone should boast" (Ephesians 2:8, 9, *NKJV*). Nevertheless, we also have a role to play in our salvation, even if that role is secondary to God's role. We must cooperate with God at every step of the process in order to complete our salvation.

God's fundamental call for us to realize our complete potential requires that we participate in what He wants to do. God has invited us to share in a divine/human

147

partnership whereby He guides and empowers us. The ultimate result of this partnership is that God helps us realize His purpose for our lives and flourish as human beings. It is a partnership in which God receives the glory and we receive the good. While eternal election means that salvation is always a free work of grace, it does not exclude God asking us to respond continuously to His gracious initiatives in our lives.

So far, so good. The question is, "How does this work?" How does God work first in our lives and then we respond to what He is doing? This chapter explores the relationship between God's gracious work in the lives of individuals and the need for those same individuals to respond to God. Throughout my discussion, I will maintain that we must cooperate with God at every level and every step of the journey. This is indeed a divine/human partnership. Our cooperation remains contingent upon the Holy Spirit's prior working and occurs primarily as we bring our choices into harmony with God's will for our lives. By gradually aligning our choices with God's choices for us, made known through the Spirit's prompting and guidance, we slowly become more holy and begin to develop the character of God.

One of the misguided ideas I have tried to address is that salvation is equal to forgiveness of sins and admittance into heaven. Instead, salvation is much broader, involving complete restoration and the full realization of all that we can become in Christ through the power of the Holy Spirit. Certainly, forgiveness is how God initiates restoration and helps us remain on the path of restoration, but that is only one dimension of salvation. If we think of salvation as a complete restoration resulting from our pursuit of holiness, we can begin to understand how it requires a process of transformation to make us more like God. We become holy and happy. We can also begin to see that our transformation as individual believers goes hand in hand with God's desire to transform the entire cosmos, creating a new heaven and a new earth. Consequently, we need to think about salvation as a journey we make—a transforming journey in which grace pushes us forward as we choose to cooperate.

THE MEDICINE OF SALVATION

There is an old illustration going back to the Middle Ages about how God works to bring about salvation in the life of every person. It stems from the idea of receiving a dose of medicine in order to cure a disease. In chapter 1, I discussed sin as a disease and the various ways it affects us. As I said then, a disease must be cured. In chapter 3, I discussed how Christ and the Spirit become the divine medicine God pours into our lives to heal us. This medicine has transforming effects when it is applied to our lives.

In the present chapter, we need to investigate the nature of our disease more carefully. While some diseases can be cured through a one-time surgery, others require a lengthy regimen of medication to restore the body to complete health. In a similar way, the salvation wrought for us by Christ and the Spirit requires a lengthy process in which the grace of God slowly restores us to complete health.

When we consider how God works to cure the disease of sin, it may be helpful to consider the way a drug works with the body. Some diseases are just too powerful for the body to fight off by itself. Our immune systems need additional help to combat certain diseases and to restore our bodies to complete health. Sometimes doctors will prescribe antibiotics to help our immune system do its job of ridding the body of infections, viruses and other diseases. In addition, we take antibiotics over a period of time and not all at once. My young daughter has battled various infections in her brief life. When the infection becomes too much for her immune system to handle, the doctor will prescribe an antibiotic that we must administer to her over a two-week period. Slowly, the antibiotic helps her body fight off the infectious disease. Although she could not overcome the infection on her own, her immune system cooperates, or works together, with the antibiotic to cure her. In this way, a partnership is created between the antibiotic and the immune system that restores the body to health and wholeness.

This illustration hints at how God works with us to cure the disease of sin. First, antibiotics empower the immune system so that it can work to heal the body. Although the immune system continues to work, it succeeds only with the prior help of the antibiotics. Likewise, God dispenses His grace to us through the work of Christ and in the power of the Spirit, thus enabling us to overcome sin. Christ and the Spirit are the divine medicine communicated in order to rid the world of sin. Christ lived a holy life, suffered, died and was raised again to redeem us from the sickness of sin and to restore us to wholeness. The Spirit conforms us to Christ by empowering us to live a holy life, helping us to die daily and, finally, resurrecting us. Only after the resurrection of our bodies will we become healed and fully whole. During this process of healing, we must cooperate with God's grace to overcome sin. We must cooperate with the Holy Spirit, who brings Christ to us and conforms our lives to Christ. However, all our cooperation is contingent on God first dispensing the required medicine.

Second, God does not cure our disease immediately. Complete healing occurs only after a long period of time in which God repeatedly administers medicine to us and we repeatedly choose to cooperate with that medicine. As I pointed out in chapter 3, conversion means more than the initial acceptance of Christ. Instead, it is a lifelong endeavor in which we attempt to become complete disciples of Christ in all we say and do. This implies that salvation includes slow healing as we work in conjunction with the Spirit to become conformed to Christ and thus free of sin's destructive power. We need daily doses of God's grace if we are to be cured completely.

We cannot die daily to sin and be made alive unto Christ Jesus without a fresh infilling of God's Spirit, who guides and enables us to choose righteousness. These daily doses of grace from the Holy Spirit bring about healing over the long haul, or our complete transformation from children of the devil to children of God. Keep in mind that God wants to make us *real* sons and daughters, not simply *legal* sons and daughters. This cannot happen without the change that comes from being conformed to the image and likeness of God's eternal Son, Jesus Christ. We conform our lives to Christ gradually as we act in cooperation with the daily dose of medicine God administers by the power of the Holy Spirit.

CHRIST AND THE SPIRIT: GOD'S TRANSFORMING MEDICINE

Examining more closely the work of Christ and the Spirit indicates how both are the divine medicine God uses to cleanse or sanctify us from the corrupting disease of sin. Our conversion to a new way of living is directly dependent on their prior work. But what is it about this work that brings our healing? Having already considered how Christ and the Spirit lead humanity on a new exodus, I now want to focus more on the Cross and resurrection of Christ in relationship to our own transformation from death to life. If we can get a clear sense of the relationship between the prior work of Christ and the Spirit and our ongoing transformation, then we will be in a better position to understand the gracious side of salvation.

All Christians agree that, on the Cross, Christ atoned

the sins of the world. Many theologians see the Cross solely as God's extension of forgiveness. To them, the work of Christ on the Cross is about forgiveness and no more. While it is important to see the Cross as the place where Jesus endured the penalty for sin, we could view it from a different perspective by asking a different set of questions: Is there a relationship between the penalty for sin and the disease of sin? How does Christ's atonement cure us from the disease of sin? What is it about the death of Christ that supplies our cure? Is there some way in which God administers healing medicine by the Cross?

Paul's claim that "For our sake [God] made him who knew no sin to be sin so that in him we might *Divine* become the righteousness of God" (2 Corinthians 5:21) *Exchange* is a good place to begin addressing these questions. Paul clearly finds an exchange between Christ and the sinner in which Christ became sin so that the sinner "in him" can become righteous. What does Paul mean by Christ becoming sin? At minimum, we can claim that Christ became sin on the Cross. While this claim helps us rule out a sinful life, it does not address what it means to say that the sinless Christ became sin.

Paul's explanation in Romans 6 provides a clue. The chapter addresses how Christ's death frees believers from slavery to sin. For Paul, sin enslaves human beings because it functions as an internal power preventing them from doing what they should. As I mentioned previously, when Paul describes sin as an internal power that reigns through corrupt desires, we should think of a disease. With this in mind, we can better understand Paul when he says, "Now if we died with Christ, we believe that we shall also live with Him, knowing that Christ, having been raised from the dead, dies no more. Death no longer has dominion over Him. For the death that He died, He died to sin once for all; but the life that He lives, He lives to God" (vv. 8-10, *NKJV*). The climax of these verses is verse 10, where Paul says that Christ died to sin once for all and now lives for God. Christ ends the grip of sin on humanity through His own death.[1]

All those who now participate in Christ's death ("if we died with Christ") begin to share His life-giving power and are made free from sin's enslavement. This suggests that Paul believes Christ experienced the full fury of the disease on the Cross because He died. The claim that Christ became sin in 2 Corinthians 5:21 is Paul's assertion that, on the Cross, Christ became subject to the consequences, or wages, of sin (see v. 23).[2] He broke the power of sin by participating in the disease itself and experiencing its ultimate consequences. As Isaiah 53 suggests, "He was wounded for our transgressions, He was bruised for our iniquities . . . and He bore the sin of many" (vv. 5, 12, *NKJV*). Romans 6 indicates that the death of Christ was about His triumph over the disease of sin by taking it upon Himself.

The book of Hebrews puts forward a similar idea about Christ's death. The writer argues in chapters 9 and 10 that Christ's sacrificial death is superior to the sacrifices of the Old Testament because it "perfects" believers by "cleansing their consciences" once and for all (9:14; 10:2, 10, 14). He explains what it means to have one's conscience cleansed by asserting that Christ's death removes consciousness of sin (10:2). The healing effect of the death of Christ involves removing an awareness of an individual's sins.[3]

Christ's blood not only becomes the channel of God's forgiveness, but that forgiveness erases the guilt experienced for past sins. The purpose of this removal is to provide confidence to worship God through prayer, praise and a lifetime of obedience (see 10:19-25; 13:15, 16). By removing the barrier that blocks true worship, which is the guilt we experience as a result of our awareness of past sins, Christ's death begins the healing process.

While removal of our awareness of sin is the primary focus of Hebrews, it is not the only healing effect of Christ's death the writer highlights. He also states, "For by one offering He has perfected forever those who are *being* sanctified" (10:14, *NKJV*, emphasis mine). Christ's sacrifice not only initially "perfects" believers for worship by cleansing the conscience, it also has ongoing effects in those who are "being sanctified." How does Christ's death continue to sanctify? The writer immediately quotes Jeremiah 31:33, 34 to suggest that, through Christ, God is writing His law upon the hearts of believers and remembering their sins no more (Hebrews 10:15-17).

There are two healing effects of Christ's death. The

Two effects of healing
Cleansed conscience
Holiness: The Beauty of Perfection
New heart created

first is immediate (cleansing the conscience), which removes any barrier on the part of the believer, while the second is ongoing (creating a new heart). These two effects are bound up with one another: God begins to create a new heart by removing our own awareness of our sins, and then He continues that work. Both are a result of the sanctifying presence of the blood of Christ.

Life in the Blood

The importance of Christ's blood sacrifice has to do with the life of God. In Leviticus 17:11, God prohibits the Israelites from eating meat with blood because "the life of the flesh is in the blood and I have assigned it to you for making expiation for your lives upon the altar."[4] The verse continues, "It is the blood, as life, that effects expiation."[5] God required blood sacrifices because blood symbolized the transferral of life. The life of the animal was exchanged for the life of the person. This transferral of life suggests that the very life of God was being poured out for us in the shedding of Christ's blood. His blood has a sanctifying effect because it is the way God communicates His life to us. As His blood covers our sinful conscience, it heals, cleanses and removes the disease of sin along with all accompanying guilt. The hymn, "The Blood Will Never Lose Its Power," captures well the idea that Christ's blood is the channel of God's powerful life, healing us in the midst of our weaknesses.

What are we to make of all this? Christ's death heals us from the disease of sin by breaking its power, cleansing our conscience and gradually creating in us a new heart. The love of God, communicated in and through the Cross, brings about the healing of the nations, and the healing of the disease of sin. To cure sin fully, Christ had to take sin upon Himself and destroy it. Guilt is a symptom of the disease. If God were simply to treat our guilt, it would be like trying to cure pneumonia in a person with AIDS. The deeper problem is AIDS, not pneumonia. Pneumonia is simply an effect of AIDS. In the same way, guilt is an effect of sin. For God to heal us, He must do more than remove the symptom, He must deal with the underlying disease.

Before dealing with the deeper disease, doctors must correct the symptoms. Pneumonia itself is a serious problem that must be treated. Any doctor knows that he must take care of the pneumonia so that the patient can be strong enough to endure the treatment for AIDS. While AIDS remains the underlying cause, pneumonia is the immediate threat that must be dealt with. On the Cross, Christ certainly was dealing with guilt as a serious symptom of our disease, but His primary mission was (and is) to cure the disease. Without the disease of sin prompting us to engage in sinful and self-destructive behavior, there would be no guilt. The Cross does not simply concern the removal of guilt. Instead, it is about God absorbing our sin into His life and destroying it by the power of that life.

Consider the example of AIDS again. If I were sick with HIV/AIDS, I would not want my father to be injected with the virus just to show me how much he loved me. However, if my father had a special property in his immune system that would allow him to build up the appropriate antibodies to defeat the disease, once injected with HIV, I could understand why he would undertake the ordeal, even if it meant great pain and suffering on his part. If, through his own torment and pain, he was actually defeating the virus and providing a cure so that I could defeat it, then his action would not only display the depth of his love for me, but it would also become the means of my own healing.

This is what Christ's death accomplishes for us. It is not simply a magnificent display of divine love, but it also represents the power of God to take our disease and suffering upon Himself and destroy it. No wonder Paul could say of God's love: "For I am convinced that neither death, nor life, nor angels, nor rulers, nor things present, nor things to come, nor powers, nor height, nor depth, nor anything else in all creation, will be able to separate us from the love of God in Christ Jesus our Lord" (Romans 8:38, 39).

As important as the death of Christ is, it cannot be separated from His life and resurrection. The remedy for our disease is not simply the death of Christ, but His life, death *and* resurrection. We know that God's medicine works because Christ's assuming our sinful disease ends with His triumphant resurrected life, not His death. The resurrection of Christ confirms that the life of God is indeed pouring forth in and through Christ. God's life is our antidote. It is the cure because His life powerfully overcomes all things. Moreover, God pours His life into us by the Holy Spirit, who is the Spirit of life. The very same Spirit of God, who raised Christ from the dead by pouring out God's own divine power, now works in believers empowering them to live and overcome. Christ's resurrection shows how the eternal Son and the eternal Spirit of God are the divine medicine who communicate God's life.

Paul writes, "If Christ is in you, the body is dead because of sin, but the Spirit is life because of righteousness. But if the Spirit of Him who raised Jesus from the dead dwells in you, He who raised Christ from the dead will also give life to your mortal bodies through His Spirit who dwells in you" (vv. 10, 11, *NKJV*). This is the connection between the work of Christ and the Spirit. If the final end of sin is death, then the ultimate cure must be new life, or new creation. In this passage, Paul asserts that God was working to cure humanity in Christ's death on the Cross and in raising Christ from the dead by means of the Holy Spirit. The remedy is nothing less than God's own life pouring forth into our lives and reviving us.

Paul goes on to declare that we have the "first fruits of the Spirit" (v. 23), which means that the Spirit is our guarantee that God's life is at work in us. This same Spirit was at work in Christ, raising Him from the dead and making Him the "first fruits of those who have died" (1 Corinthians 15:20). If Paul tells us that the Spirit is the "down payment" for the cure, he also wants us to see that this cure culminates in our own bodily resurrection. In the end, we will be fully healed when "death is swallowed up in victory," because "this corruptible must put on incorruption and this mortal must put on immortality" (vv. 53, 54, *NKJV*). The end of the process of transformation is resurrection. Until we arrive at that point, the Spirit of life works in us, helping us to die to sin. God's cure centers on the work of Christ and the Spirit because they are the exclusive dispensers of the divine medicine, which cures us of the disease of sin and all its effects.

When we see how God cures us, we realize that salvation is a work of grace. How can we be cured if we do not have the proper medicine? Although our spiritual immune systems arc unable to overcome the powerful effects of sin, we can participate in God's cure. Since salvation is about our complete transformation from a person diseased by sin to one healed by grace, our cooperation is essential to that transformation.

How God Dispenses the Medicine

As God's spiritual antibiotic, the work of Christ and the Spirit still must be applied to individuals. This leads to another set of issues concerning how God dispenses this medicine to us. How do we cooperate with God while salvation remains a work of undeserved grace? How can we make any choice to embrace God's cure since we are diseased?

The simple explanation is that the Spirit enables us to choose. John's Gospel indicates that to be born again is to be born of the Spirit (3:5-8). It is the Spirit who gives birth to the new life Christians begin to experience in Christ. The Spirit initiates new birth by convicting the world of sin (16:8, 9) and awakening people to the reality that they are indeed diseased. To put it in Paul's terms, the Spirit must remove the veil by which the god of this world has blinded people's hearts (2 Corinthians 3:12—4:6). The blindness produced by sinful patterns of behavior prevents people from recognizing the need to be cured. In the same way that an alcoholic must first be convinced that he has a problem, sinners must be convinced that they are diseased. The Spirit must also give individuals the power to choose. It is one thing to recognize the truth, but it is quite another to act on it. The Spirit must help us do both.

Before moving any further in our discussion, let me make a simple but important point. God leaves no one out when dispensing His medicine. Everyone gets a dose. The Bible declares, "God so loved the world that He gave His only begotten Son, that whoever believes in Him should not perish but have everlasting life" (John 3:16, *NKJV*). The Gospel writer indicates that God extends salvation to everyone. The pronoun *whoever* implies that God gives His medicine to the entire world. The call to salvation is a universal call that goes out to every person.

One could object that if God dispenses His medicine to everyone, then everyone must be saved. Not at all. It should be clear by now that salvation is about our complete healing, which means that one dose of medicine will not suffice. The claim that God dispenses His medicine to everyone means that God gives the initial dose freely to all.

John Wesley referred to the initial dose as *prevenient*

grace because he thought God supplied some grace beforehand to enable us to choose Him.[6] This does not imply that everyone chooses to cooperate with God. Some receive the initial dose and then decide that they don't need any more. If salvation depends upon our cooperation, then we can choose not to cooperate. We can refuse God's treatment.

Let me return to the medicine illustration to make the point clearer. Imagine that God walked into a hospital filled with terminally ill patients. Their diseases are so progressed that they have lost consciousness. What is God's response? Does God wait for them to respond to Him, knowing they cannot regain consciousness on their own? Or, does God give them an initial dose of medicine? The doctrine of prevenient grace implies the latter. Instead of waiting for people to do something they cannot do, God invites the entire world to receive His cure. He takes the initiative and administers the first dose of medicine.

What does the first dose accomplish? It restores consciousness to the patients so that they can see and understand their condition. They also understand that they require *additional* doses of medicine to complete their treatment. Since salvation is about complete transformation, it requires long-term treatment. The initial dose is to get the patient to the point where a choice is possible. Is the patient compelled to continue treatment? No. The cure is offered, but the patient must decide periodically to receive God's medicine. He or she must die daily to sin and be made alive unto righteousness, which requires asking God for additional doses every day.

While my explanation illustrates how God dispenses the initial dose, it does not indicate where this happens. Can we point to real-life scenarios where God is actually dispensing His medicine? One of the best examples is what happens every Sunday morning as pastors deliver their sermons. Pastors are clear examples of ambassadors through whom God makes His appeal to the world and dispenses His medicine (see 2 Corinthians 5:20).

When pastors deliver sermons on Sunday mornings, they are attempting to communicate the message of the gospel to their audiences. The problem is that no pastor can communicate the gospel in such a way that it connects to every individual in the audience. Even in a church of 50 people, it is almost impossible to preach a sermon that will resonate with every one of them. Every person is dealing with different issues and most sermons cannot address every issue. Most pastors recognize that even their best sermons may not reach anyone. Sometimes people just don't respond.

To understand how people respond to a sermon, we need to consider the work of the Spirit. When a message goes forth from the pulpit, it takes on a life of its own because the Spirit begins to work in and through the message. While it is impossible for a human being to communicate a message that will speak to 50 individuals, it is certainly possible for the Spirit. The Spirit knows the inner thoughts of each heart and is fully capable of applying a sermon to every situation, even if the pastor is not.

One phrase from the lips of a pastor can penetrate the heart of a particular person if the Spirit is at work. One phrase like "God is sovereign," may impact an individual more than anything else the pastor says. Theologians have described this as the difference between the external call of God and the internal call of God. The external call has to do with the sermon that goes forth from the pulpit and exists outside of the hearer. The internal call refers to the word that the Spirit speaks inside the mind of the hearer. The Spirit empowers the listener to choose by applying the message to his or her life in a way that resonates with the issues he or she is facing. The individual responds because the phrase, "God is sovereign," speaks to the lack of control he or she senses. This is the work of the Holy Spirit dispensing God's medicine.

Have you ever had a moment of insight in your own life? Was there a time when you came to see the truth about who you are and what you need? What generates this moment of insight? The Spirit inspires these moments of insight by working in our hearts to open our eyes so that we can see the truth. This happens through sermons, but it can also happen in other ways. It can even happen when a friend gives us a piece of advice. God uses all kinds of things to awaken us to the truth about our condition. When we have these moments of insight, we have a choice. We can choose to act on them or not. We can choose to receive the dose of medicine God is giving or refuse the treatment. When we choose to live in light of the truth that God communicates to us, we are saying, "God, I accept Your medicine and I want more."

HOW WE RESPOND TO THE MEDICINE

Although God is always actively at work in our lives, attempting to bring us to Christ, the journey of salvation begins the moment we cooperate with the work of the Holy Spirit. Following scripture, we can refer to this moment of cooperation as the *act of faith*. When individuals "believe on the Lord Jesus Christ," that is, when they exercise faith in Christ, they are cooperating with the work of the Spirit. We embrace Christ by faith alone, and we remain connected to Christ by faith alone.

What does it mean to exercise faith? What are we doing when we believe in Christ for our salvation? Early Protestant theologians described the act of faith as trust in God or heartfelt reliance upon God. To rely on anyone is to place yourself and your well-being into the hands of another, which is always a risky venture. Sometimes the risk is minimal, while other times the risk is great. I rely on the postal worker to deliver my mail, but if he fails to do so, the cost to me is inconvenience more than anything else. However, when a person with a life-threatening disease visits a doctor, she places her life in his hands, relying upon his medical knowledge and expertise to cure her. To trust God for salvation is the greatest risk of all. It means placing one's personal destiny and spiritual well-being into God's hands. Believing in Christ for salvation first involves a reliance or trust upon Christ to do what we cannot do: heal us of the self-destructive choices resulting from the disease of sin.

When Paul tells us to believe in Jesus for salvation (Romans 10:9), he wants us to trust Christ to save us. This leads us to the second part of the act of faith. It is a heartfelt reliance upon Christ. The term *heartfelt* means the commitment to rely on Christ must be total. The famous Protestant Reformer, Martin Luther, describes heartfelt reliance by relating it to the idea of getting on a ship.[7] Luther wants us to consider what it means to step foot on a ship and *trust* it to carry us across an ocean so that we arrive safely on the other side. The moment we put both feet on the ship is the moment we begin to trust. This trust is total. We are placing our lives in the hands of the crew running this large piece of machinery. Will the ship do what the captain claims it will do? Will it get us to the other side of the ocean? This is what it means to have heartfelt reliance. It is when we are invested in God's work. When the ship leaves the dock we know that its journey and our journeys must be made together.

It would be a mistake to think of the act of faith as a onetime decision. We must trust that God is indeed at work in our lives, curing us of the disease of sin even when this does not seem to be the case. Both the initial choice to believe and the ongoing response of belief should characterize our lives as Christians if we are to be transformed. We must trust God because although salvation is a gradual process, it is not always one of forward movement. It's more like two steps forward and one step backward. Only when we view the process from the end can we see that we were progressively inching our way toward perfection.

In the middle of the journey, it can become difficult to tell what God is doing because the journey itself is filled with starts and stops, failures and successes. From beginning to end, we must see what God is doing with the eyes of faith. Hebrews makes it clear that "faith is the assurance of things hoped for, the conviction of things not seen" (11:1). Only when the process is over will faith give way to full sight. We will no longer see through a mirror darkly but will see God face-to-face. Until then, we must work with all of His energy which so powerfully energizes us (Colossians 1:29).

SUMMARY

The cooperation between human freedom and divine grace is at the heart of salvation. Salvation remains a work of grace because God develops and dispenses the divine medicine by the work of Christ and the Spirit. This medicine is the very power of God's indestructible life being given to us. We must respond if we are to be saved completely.

We cannot realize our complete potential as human beings apart from God, but neither can we realize it apart from the exercise of our choice. Each time we respond to God's medicine, we are trusting Him to do what He has promised. One day, we will put on immortality and incorruption. One day, we will see God. Until then, we must work because God works in us and through us.

ENDNOTES

[1] See J. Ziesler, *Paul's Letter to the Romans*, TPI New Testament Commentaries (Philadelphia: Trinity, 1989) 161, 162.

[2] J. Murphy-O'Connor, *The Theology of the Second Letter to the Corinthians* (Cambridge: Cambridge UP, 1991) 61, 62.

[3] See David A. Peterson, *Hebrews and Perfection: An Examination of the Concept of Perfection in the Epistle to the Hebrews* (Cambridge: Cambridge UP, 1982) 140, 166, 167; and Harold W. Attridge, *Hebrews* (Philadelphia: Fortress, 1989) 280, 281.

[4] *Tanakh: The Holy Scriptures, The New JPS Translation According to the Traditional Hebrew Text* (Philadelphia: Jewish Publication Society, 1988).

[5] *Tanakh.*

[6] See Wesley's sermon, "On Working Out Your Own Salvation," in *John Wesley's Sermons: An Anthology*, ed. A.C. Outler and R.P. Heitzenrater (Nashville, TN: Abingdon, 1991) 485-492. For an explanation of Wesley's doctrine of prevenient grace, see Kenneth J. Collins, *The Scripture Way of Salvation: The Heart of John Wesley's Theology* (Nashville, TN: Abingdon, 1997) 38-45.

[7] See Alister E. McGrath, *Reformation Thought: An Introduction*, 3rd ed. (Oxford: Blackwell, 1999) 111, 112.

PART III

THE PURSUIT OF HOLINESS

CHAPTER 7

Setting the Heart on Fire

As the deer pants for the water brooks,
so pants my soul for You, O God.
My soul thirsts for God, for the living God
(Psalm 42: 1, 2, *NKJV*).

When we consider how salvation necessitates our complete transformation from a person diseased by sin to one healed by grace, we are immediately struck with a potential problem. Anyone who has embarked on a long journey knows that completing the journey requires a great deal of effort and determination. Along the way are numerous obstacles to overcome. Some obstacles come from inside, such as when we make wrong choices. Other obstacles come from outside, such as when we lose someone we love, encounter discrimination because of race or gender, experience conflict in our relationships with others or face life changes like having children, getting laid off, and so forth.

These obstacles conspire against us, making the journey much more difficult to complete. Sometimes we wonder if the journey is worth all the pain and anguish we experience. In the midst of these obstacles, we must possess the determination and stamina to stay on course. As Paul reminds us, many runners compete in a race, but only one gets the prize (1 Corinthians 9:24). Like Paul, we must run to get the prize.

How do we press on and maintain that determination of will that says, "Victory shall be mine!"? Even with God's help, pursuing holiness is difficult. Anyone who thinks differently is either foolish or has never tried to live a holy life. When Paul declares that he presses on toward the goal to win the prize (Philippians 3:14), the journey he is describing is long and demanding. Paul's message of salvation by grace does not exempt him from the difficult work of daily dying to himself and becoming alive to Christ in holiness.

To overcome the obstacles that impede us, we must allow God continuously to set our hearts on fire with renewed energy. This is a fire of passion that propels us onward and upward in our quest to see God and finish the race. It's the passion expressed in Paul's declaration that "whatever gains I had, these I have come to regard as loss because of Christ" (Philippians 3:7,). It's the passion of the psalmist who cries out, "For a day in your courts is better than a thousand elsewhere. I would rather be a doorkeeper in the house of my God than live in the tents of wickedness" (Psalm 84:10). It's the passion of a bride who longs for her bridegroom. This passion not only inflames the heart, but melts it and makes it one with Christ. In short, it helps us to fulfill the commandment to love the Lord your God with all of your heart, soul, mind and strength.

In this chapter, I want to examine how holy passion supplies the fuel that helps us pursue holiness in the midst of the difficult journey of salvation. I also want to explain how we can cultivate our passion for God.

HOLY PASSION AS THE FUEL OF A HOLY LIFE

When we view salvation as a transforming journey and a passionate longing for God, it leads us to the marriage between Christ and the believer, or the bride and her heavenly Bridegroom (cf. Ephesians 5:21-33; Revelation 19:7; 21:2, 9; 22:17).

Marriage is a lifelong journey of two people who seek to intertwine their hearts and make them one. This goal is not accomplished easily or quickly. Both partners must work hard at learning to love one another, which requires that both partners grow and change. In a certain sense, both partners must die to their old ways of single living and embrace new ways of living together as a couple. What helps fuel the hard work of marriage is the fire of passion each partner has for the other. This passion helps to consummate their love and solidify it in a long-term commitment. Scripture describes this in terms of a covenant.

I am not implying that this passion is, or even should be, present all the time. *Passion* is a temporary period of intense emotional activity in which emotions explode outward in attraction to someone or something else. Sometimes passion erupts spontaneously and unexpectedly, while at other times it bubbles up from intentional actions on the part of the married couple. Regardless, all couples need to rekindle their passion for one another from time to time in order to further develop a long-term loving disposition.

Rekindling passion does not mean just sexual passion. Couples should be reminded of the qualities that attracted them to one another and notice new qualities that emerge in the course of each person's growth and development. Sometimes this happens in simple ways. For example, when I see my wife standing her ground in a debate over a woman's role in the home or in ministry, I am reminded of how attractive I find her courage and strength of mind. Her refusal to be consigned to a certain stereotype of women is one of the reasons why I am so passionately committed to her. Seeing her courage in action sparks my passion for her and prompts me to draw closer to her. At other times, couples must be intentional about rekindling their passion by setting aside special times to spend together. In these ways passion fuels a marriage and enables both partners to press through the difficult times and the hard work of becoming one in heart and mind.

Our relationship with Christ works in a similar way. As Scripture indicates, we are being united to Christ in marriage by the Spirit. While the final consummation of this marriage awaits Christ's second coming, as Paul makes clear in Ephesians 5, it is also a present reality for believers. To make this marriage between Christ and the believer last over time, it must be fueled with passion. However, there are important differences between human marriages and the marriage between Christ and the believer. In human marriages, both partners must learn to love one another, which requires that each change and adapt. In the marriage between Christ and the believer, Christ always remains fully committed to the believer. Believers are the ones who must change and adapt as they learn to love and cleave to Christ.

Johann von Staupitz (d. 1524), one of Martin Luther's teachers, helps us see that what keeps us committed to Christ is the love of the Spirit inflaming our hearts and moving us closer and closer toward God. Staupitz suggests that this love does not make *us* pleasing to God, but *God* pleasing to us. He states that believers are . . . "made alive through faith active in love: that is to say, active through the fire of our love, set afire by the love of Him who is the only perpetual fire, coming down from heaven. All other fires have lost their spell. This fire makes God pleasing and acceptable to us, so that not only what is contrary to God but also that which is not God becomes displeasing to us. . . . Through this love we are and live upright and just, not for ourselves but for God."[1]

The fire of holiness urges us forward in our quest to know God more intimately. Staupitz captures that Pentecostal passion for holiness by referencing its origin in the love of God shed abroad in the heart of the believer by the power and presence of the Holy Spirit. Notice where Staupitz locates the problem. It is not with God's attitude to the believer, which remains loving;

rather, the obstacle resides within the believer, who must learn to see God as pleasing and acceptable, someone to pursue with the whole heart, soul, mind and strength.

Cultivating a Passon for God

Corporate Worship Cultivates Passion

The Pentecostal power to overcome sin, death, disease and the devil comes from the fiery passion of a heart set ablaze by the Holy Spirit. It is the power to press on and say in the words of the old hymn,

> On Christ the solid Rock I stand
> All other ground is sinking sand
> All other ground is sinking sand.

My use of a song to illustrate this point is intentional because worship is one of the primary ways our hearts are set ablaze. Thanksgiving, prayer and praise all contribute to the creation of holy passion. As we worship God, particularly in a worship service, the Spirit helps us bend all of our longings and desires toward heaven. How does that happen? When we enter into the songs of worship, we are reminded of who God is and what He has done for us. Worship songs and hymns paint a picture of God that brings into focus God's own characteristics, helping us to see that God is indeed our ultimate good. As the fuel of a holy life, passion evoked by these songs or hymns helps us develop an affection for God, removing any spiritual paralysis that may beset us and pushing us toward perfection.

Let me illustrate further how worship helps us rekindle holy passion with something that happened to me one Sunday morning when my church was singing the worship chorus, "I See the Lord." The song summarizes Isaiah's vision of God in Isaiah 6. As I sang the words that morning, I found myself focusing on the Isaiah passage and rehearsing the nature of this majestic God seated upon His throne. I pondered the description of God's robe filling the Temple, which conveys the sovereignty and stateliness of the ruler of all Creation. For a moment, caught up in Isaiah's vision, I beheld an image of the majesty and glory of the Lord who sovereignly reigns over the earth with perfect power and perfect justice. I saw the One who cannot sin, who always acts uprightly, who delivers His people from their sins, who hears the widow's cries and who is working all things together for the good of His Creation.

Reflecting on the words of the song, I turned them into a prayer:

Prayer & Praise come together

Lord, let the whole earth be filled with Your glory. Lord, let this kingdom that You have established with Your power and might fill the earth, consuming injustice, bringing peace, causing the lion to lie down with the lamb and restoring everything to its rightful place for Your glory. Lord, let this kingdom be established in me; may I reflect Your glory and majesty in my life for You are majestic and wondrous to behold.

All of this occurred in only a few moments, but it

inflamed my heart. I left that service in love with my God all over again and determined to pursue Him and the establishment of His kingdom at all costs. This is how prayer and praise can come together to form worship, and it is one way our hearts become inflamed for God, the object of our love. In addition, this is the work of the Holy Spirit.

As we worship, the Spirit pours Himself into our hearts and catches us away into a vision of God. We leave worship with a renewed passion for God and His kingdom, our hearts having been wedded to His heart once again, and determined to pursue holiness in our life, our church and our world.

When we enter into public worship, we learn to love God by having our passions for Him ignited once again. The hymn, "Here is Love," written by the Welshman William Rees (d. 1883) provides a good example:

> Here is love, vast as the ocean;
> Lovingkindness as the flood.
> When the Prince of Life, our ransom
> Shed for us His precious blood.
> Who His love will not remember?
> Who can cease to sing His praise?
> He can never be forgotten
> Throughout heav'n's eternal days.
>
> On the mount of Crucifixion,
> Fountains opened deep and wide.
> Through the floodgates of God's mercy
> Flowed a vast and gracious tide.
> Grace and love, like mighty rivers
> Poured incessant from above,

And heav'n's peace and perfect justice
Kissed a guilty world in love.

The hymn attempts to arouse our passion for God by reminding us of what Christ has done for us on the Cross. In this sense, it is similar to how husbands and wives stir their passion for one another. In the same way that I am moved with passion for my wife when I see her standing her ground in debate, my heart is moved toward God when I remember all that He has done for me in Christ.

While public worship can rekindle our passions for God, there is no automatic guarantee that it will happen every time. We must approach worship in the same way we approach every other aspect of our relationship with Christ: with faith, hope and love. As we lift our voices in song, we must believe that the Holy Spirit will make Christ present to us through the words. When we sing the words, we must hope in eager expectation for the coming of our King. We must draw on the deep reservoir of God's love for us, asking the Spirit, who pours this love into our hearts, to raise us above ourselves even as Christ descends to us. By exercising faith, hope and love, we prepare ourselves to receive Christ, even on those days when our passions are not ignited.

INTIMACY AS THE HEART OF WORSHIP

While corporate worship offers one place to renew passion for God, the act of worship is much broader than what happens in a service. Broadly speaking, worship

worship is ...

may be defined as "a prayerful posture that finds in God the ultimate fulfillment of all that we are." Good posture refers to the way the vertebrae in an individual's back all become aligned in the correct position. In the same way, good spiritual posture is when our desires become fixed upon God. In Sonnet 116, Shakespeare defines true love as fixing one's desires upon another person so that they cannot be shaken.

> Love is not love
> Which alters when it alteration finds,
> Or bends with the remover to remove:
> O no! it is an ever-fixed mark
> That looks on tempests and is never shaken.

Love does not alter or change, even when the person who is loved changes; nor does love cease or change when it is not returned. For Shakespeare, the power of true love lies in its being "an ever-fixed mark" that does not waver through the changes of life. True love implies a covenant in which one person fixes his desires upon another and refuses to be moved. It is the posture an individual has or the stand that he takes when he declares, "I will love *you* and no other." This is what it means to fix one's desires.

Fixing our desires upon God involves the development of a way of thinking about God and the realization that our lives find their ultimate fulfillment in God. Worship is a prayerful posture because it involves a constant mind-set or attitude that causes us to cleave to our heavenly Bridegroom. "I will love you, Lord, and no other god." Central to the development of this mind-set is a drive to cultivate intimacy with God, which is fueled by setting our hearts on fire with holy passion.

When one person wants to be with another, he or she desires to move into an intimate relationship with that person. There are two Scriptures, in particular, that describe the intimate relationship between God and the believer and provide insight into the nature of worship as a prayerful posture.

The first text is found at the end of Revelation where John writes: "And the Spirit and the bride say, 'Come!' And let him who hears say, 'Come!' And let him who thirsts come. Whoever desires, let him take the water of life freely" (22:17, *NKJV*).

In his book on Revelation, Richard Bauckham identifies two important aspects to this passage.[2] First, the bride identified here is the New Jerusalem, which means the church as she will be at the end of time and not the church in her present state (cf. Revelation 21:2).

Second, John invites his readers, including the seven churches of Asia, to be part of this bride if they will join in the prayer for the bridegroom to come. As John reminds each of the seven churches, "Listen to what the Spirit is saying." The Spirit is saying "Come!" Each church, and therefore each believer, is invited to join her voice to the Spirit's.

Believers engage in worship when, as the Bride of Christ, they can say to their Bridegroom with all of our heart, "Come!" The prayer for the Bridegroom to come expresses the ardent desire of a bride to unite to her beloved, her first love. It is the language of love that stands behind the request and, as John makes clear, the Spirit inspires this language. To yearn for the coming of the Bridegroom is to recognize that one's life will find its completion in the divine embrace with Christ. This is how we begin to fix our desires upon God. We ground our longing for Christ's return in our desire to be with Christ, to be in His presence.

The same point could also be made about the Abba cry. Believers engage in worship when they can say to God with all of our heart, "Abba! Father!" The "Abba cry" reveals another way to fix our desires upon God by expressing the intimate bond between a child and her father. We are children of the Father of Jesus Christ. As Paul indicates, "God has sent the Spirit of his Son into our hearts crying, 'Abba! Father!'" (Galatians 4:6, emphasis mine).

Paul makes a similar point in Romans 8:14-16 where he states, "As many as are led by the Spirit of God, these are the sons of God. For you did not receive the spirit of bondage again to fear, but you receive the Spirit of adoption by whom we cry out, 'Abba, Father.' The Spirit Himself bears witness with our spirit that we are the children of God" (*NKJV*).

Gordon Fee suggests that Paul's choice of "Spirit of his Son" in Galatians is no mistake. It indicates to the believer that the Spirit causes her to share in the intimate relationship between Jesus and the Father.[3] Jesus himself addressed God as "Abba," and the fact that we, inspired by the Spirit, can utter those words is a sign of the intimate relationship God has established with us and the need for us to mature in that relationship. God wants us to know that we are His children and He has poured forth His Spirit as a sign to us of our adoption into His family. Those who respond to the Spirit's prompting with the cry, "Abba! Father!" see God as having all that they need.

My daughter has a peculiar behavior when she wants to get close to her mother or me. Like all children, sometimes she experiences separation anxiety and needs to be reassured that we are there for her. Sometimes she just wants to express her affection for us and her need to have us close. During these moments, she will bury her face in my wife's face or my face, placing her forehead against mine and slowly rocking her head from side to side like a skater performing a figure eight. In this brief display of affection, there is no need for an exchange of words. The actions clearly communicate my daughter's desire to be intimate with us, her parents.

As she grows and matures, she will change the way she displays affection, but I hope she will always desire to do so. I think the Abba cry embodies both God's desire for us to display affection for Him and our own wish to express affection for our heavenly Father. Our displays of affection will change as we change and the cry "Abba!" will be expressed differently.

There may be times in our lives where we need to bury our faces in God's, slowly rocking our heads as His Spirit envelops us in the loving embrace of the

Father. At other times, we may indicate how much we love God by performing good works such as evangelizing, taking care of the sick or helping the oppressed. However we express such affection, it is the affection itself that encompasses the heart of worship.

Come Now is the time to Worship

Both "Abba! Father!" and "Come!" can easily be trivialized or overlooked, but they take on different meanings when uttered by a person who desires God. The difference has to do with the posture of the person speaking the words. Someone who is in love with another human being and is passionately devoted to that person would not see the request to "come" as trivial. Instead, the request symbolizes that person's deep commitment and desire to be with his beloved.

There have been times when my wife and I were separated for long periods of time because of my education. During those times, she has said, "I wish you would come home," or I have said, "I wish I could come home." The wish to come home to the other expresses our desire to be with one another and helps us continue to fix our desires upon one another. It is one of the ways we develop a posture of love toward each other.

The same is true of "Abba! Father!" The phrase captures a person's desire to express fully the deep commitment of a child for a father. When Paul indicates that we cry out "Abba! Father!" by the Holy Spirit, he seems to be suggesting that the depth of commitment evident in the cry cannot occur apart from the Spirit's work. In crying out to God, we are learning to fix our desires upon Him as the one who has all of the answers to life's questions. We cannot express this deep commitment to God in words unless the Spirit is actively igniting our love. The Spirit inflames our hearts to invite the Lord Jesus to come and cry "Abba! Father!"

Now, let's bring our brief examination of these passages full circle and look at how they reinforce my definition of worship. Remember, worship is a prayerful posture that finds in God the ultimate fulfillment of all that we are. If we consider both passages in the context of our relationship with God, they indicate how we present ourselves as living sacrifices (Romans 12:1, 2). Living sacrifices are believers who dedicate their lives wholly to God, because they find the completion of their life in Him ("In him we live and move and have our being," Acts 17:28) and long to be with God. In worship, we fix our desires upon God by longing for Christ to come and by crying out "Abba! Father!"

Prayer Cultivates Intimacy

Describing worship as a "prayerful posture" conveys how prayer cultivates worship by helping us develop good posture toward God. While prayer can take on a petitionary tone, the primary reason for prayer is not asking God for an answer to every question. Instead, the purpose of prayer is the cultivation of intimacy with God. Prayer means spending time with Christ, learning more about Him and growing closer to Him.

Conforming our lives to Christ requires that we cultivate the intimacy necessary to know Christ, and this intimacy begins with prayer. This is how prayer develops a prayerful posture that leads to worship. It is in the context of prayer that we say "Come" and cry out "Abba! Father!" As Richard Foster put it, prayer is the way to "find the heart's true home."[4] As we cultivate intimacy with God in prayer, we develop a posture of prayer that points us heavenward and keeps us focused on Christ, even in the midst of the daily affairs of life.

How do we draw closer to Christ through prayer? How do we cultivate the intimacy needed to develop a prayerful posture? Christians constantly talk about spending time in God's presence, but what do they mean? How can we have a conversation with God that is a true dialogue? Let me offer at least two ways to foster dialogue with God.

1. *We dialogue with God by praying through our theology.* This means praying what we believe about God, Christ, the Holy Spirit and other doctrines, such as those found in the Church of God Declaration of Faith or other statements of faith. Whether we recognize it or not, all Christians have a theology because all Christians believe certain things about God, Jesus, the Spirit, salvation, and so forth. Although our theology should be grounded upon Scripture, it is not reducible to the Scriptures themselves. There is a clear difference between Biblical studies and theology. Biblical studies attempts to understand the concerns of the Biblical authors in the context of their own time, whereas theology emerges the moment we bring our own questions to the Scriptures.

James Dobson's book on dealing with a strong-willed child asks a 21st-century question, not a first-century question. To answer this question, he must engage in theology (with a little child psychology thrown in), not Biblical studies. He claims that his advice on raising children is Biblical, but he means that it reflects what Scripture says.

Theology becomes Biblical when it faithfully reflects what is in Scripture. Conversely, theology is unbiblical when it does not faithfully reflect what is in Scripture. Jehovah's Witnesses may have a theology, but it is not a faithful reflection of what the Scriptures teach about God, Christ and salvation. Theology represents our understanding of who God is and what He is doing in light of the Scriptures.

Theology defined

When we pray our theology, we enter into a conversation with God. Our theology helps us construct a picture of God so that we can know something about who we are addressing in our prayers. To put it differently, what we believe about God and salvation (what God is doing for us), forms a portrait of God that helps us know something of the One to whom we pray. We do not pray to some faceless, shapeless deity—we pray to the God revealed in Jesus Christ.

In a similar way, I am married to a real person who has her own unique personality. The only way I can cultivate intimacy with my wife is by taking the time to get to know her. To do so, I must study her and get to know her personality, her likes and dislikes, her strengths and weaknesses. The more I study my wife, the more intimate our conversations become, because those conversations are based on a correct knowledge of who she really is. Likewise, we cultivate intimacy with God by taking the time to get to know Him. If we want to know something about the One to whom we are praying, we should study theology.

The simplest definition of theology is "the study of God." In the same way that I get to know my wife by studying what she does and listening to what's important to her, I get to know God by studying and finding out what's important to Him. As Karl Barth reminds us, "Prayer without study would be empty. Study without prayer would be blind."[5] My theology helps me talk to God in prayer and listen to God speak to me.

Consider for a moment the idea that God is sovereign. This truth communicates something about the nature of God. To say that God is sovereign is to understand that He is in control of all events. In addition, God is in control because He possesses perfect power and perfect wisdom; God knows exactly what to do and He has the ability to bring it to pass. It is because God is sovereign that He can work all things together for our good. Scripture describes God's sovereignty in different ways by calling God a king who rules righteously, a warrior who fights on behalf of His people, one who controls the winds and the waves, and so forth. Praying in light of the idea that God is sovereign God would go something like this:

> God, I know that You are in control of the events of my life. For You are God and there is no other, You

are God and there is no one like you (Isaiah 46:9).
You ride on the wings of wind (Psalm 18:10); You
hide me beneath the shelter of your wings (61:4); You
protect me from the storm; for you, O Lord, calm the
storm and bring peace to my life. I trust that You are
working all things together for my good (Romans
8:28) because I know that there is nothing outside of
Your control. For the eyes of the Lord survey the
earth (2 Chronicles 16:9; Zechariah 4:10) and there is
nothing hidden from them. Lord, You know my
future, there is nothing hidden from Your sight; you
see farther than I can and I know that You will do
what is right for me.

Notice that Scriptural ideas run throughout the prayer
and confirm the idea that God is sovereign. To pray this
way—filled with Scriptural ideas about God—requires
that the person engage in theology. The Scriptural ideas
fill out our view of God so that we can know not only
that God is sovereign, but we can also know what that
means. We are getting to know God.

2. *We dialogue with God by listening to the voice of
the Spirit speaking to our hearts.* The Spirit speaks in
a variety of ways. In an important sense, the Spirit
talks to us through the Scriptures, giving us a portrait
of the Father and the Son, which forms our theology.
In addition, when we pray our theology, the Spirit can
speak to us by reminding us of what God has done, or
helping us to see how God is working. Praying through
the idea that God is sovereign may help us know that
God is working, even when we cannot see what He is
doing. The Spirit may remind us that God will bring

us through a particular trial because He is sovereign and we need to trust in Him. Conversely, the Spirit may suggest that we need to allow God to exercise sovereignty over our lives by surrendering certain areas to Him.

As the Spirit convicts us or reminds us of God's work, our prayer becomes a true dialogue with God. How does this happen? Sometimes the Spirit speaks to us by giving us strong impressions about ourselves. As we pray, "God I know You are in charge of my situation," the Spirit may impress on our minds the thought that God has not left us, but He is always with us. This is one way the Spirit can bring comfort.

The Spirit can also take us to a passage of Scripture that addresses our particular situation. He may bring to mind Paul's declaration that nothing can separate us from the God's love (Romans 8:37-39), or Jesus' words "I am with you always" (Matthew 28:20, *NKJV*).

A third way the Spirit speaks is by helping us make connections between different ideas or find a meaning to a passage of Scripture that before was hidden from us. Remember the example I gave of singing the chorus based on Isaiah 6 and Isaiah's vision of God? As I sang that song, the Spirit helped me to begin to make connections between the words of the song, Isaiah's text and my own desires for God's kingdom to be established. In all of these ways and more, the Spirit speaks to us and inflames our desires for God as we pray.

SUMMARY

In this chapter, I have discussed how love for God

inflames the believer by creating holy passions for God. But this holy passion should be distinguished from a loving disposition that comes over time. As a result of their emotional intensity, sometimes people mistake passion for a loving disposition. Passion tends to be strong desires grounded upon an attraction to someone or something, whereas a loving disposition points toward a condition that causes one to cleave to another over the long haul.

We use the word love to refer both to passion and a loving disposition, but these two ideas should be kept separate. When Shakespeare declares that love is "an ever-fixed mark," he is referring to a constant disposition a person has to cling to his beloved. Passion provides an important ingredient in any loving relationship, but if that relationship is going to last, it must include more than mere passion. Since pursuing holiness is a lifelong journey of uniting ourselves to Christ in ever increasing degrees, we need determination and stamina to go the distance. This determination begins with rekindling holy passion for God and is consummated when that passion solidifies into a constant loving disposition.

We can get a clearer understanding of the difference between passion and a loving disposition by returning to the relationship between a husband and a wife. Any romance between two persons usually begins with some sort of attraction. We are initially attracted to him or her for a variety of reasons. Part of the attraction is physical—we find the person's facial features, hair style and bodily shapes and curves appealing. Another part of our attraction is the individual's personality. Whether the person is funny or serious or shares our likes or dislikes is an attraction that becomes stronger or weaker as we learn more about the individual. If the attraction grows, it can form a passion that eventually leads to marriage.

Once we move into the marital state, we must learn to combine passion for our mate with actions giving expression to that passion. For example, we take our spouse out for dinner, buy him or her nice clothes, take out the trash, mow the lawn, wash the dishes, share our hopes and dreams with him or her and a host of other actions that express how committed we are. When we combine passionate commitment with actions, we create a permanent loving disposition that causes us to cleave to that person above anyone else. Even when passions erupt in physical attraction for someone else, which happens from time to time, the loving disposition solidifies our commitment to our mate and forms the covenant framework for marriage.

Divorce can happen when couples do not always stabilize their passion for one another. This is especially the case with so-called "no-fault divorces," in which spouses simply decide they can no longer live with one another. They "fall out of love" with one another because they fail to turn their initial passion for one another into a constant loving disposition. At the end of the day, passion—even holy passion—is fleeting. While setting our hearts on fire for God helps keep us on the path of holiness, we must make that passion permanent. As we cultivate our passion for God and turn it into a loving disposition, we find ourselves running in such a way as to obtain the prize.

ENDNOTES

[1] Johann von Staupitz, *Eternal Predestination and its Execution in Time as found in Heiko Oberman, Forerunners of the Reformation: The Shape of Late Medieval Thought Illustrated by Key Documents* (Philadelphia: Fortress Press, 1981) 182, 183.

[2] Richard Bauckham, *The Climax of Prophecy: Studies on the Book of Revelation* (Edinburgh: T & T Clark, 1993) 166-168.

[3] Fee, *God's Empowering Presence*, 404ff. See also J.D.G. Dunn, "Spirit Speech: Reflections on Romans 8:12-27" in *Romans and the People of God*, 84.

[4] Richard Foster, *Prayer: Finding the Heart's True Home* (San Francisco: Harper, 1992).

[5] Karl Barth, *Evangelical Theology: An Introduction*, trans. G. Farley (Grand Rapids, MI: Eerdmans, 1979) 171.

CHAPTER 8

Fostering a Holy Life

But the fruit of the Spirit is love, joy, peace, longsuffering, kindness, goodness, faithfulness, gentleness, self-control. Against such there is no law. And those who are Christ's have crucified the flesh with its passions and desires. If we live in the Spirit, let us also walk in the Spirit (Galatians 5:22-25, NKJV).

In this chapter, I want to weave together some themes I have discussed earlier but have not developed fully. The previous chapter was devoted to sustaining our pursuit of holiness by cultivating a passion for God that more closely unites us to the eternal Bridegroom through worship and prayer. As we worship God and seek intimacy in prayer, our hearts are set aflame by the Spirit of God, which motivates us to pursue holiness.

The present chapter explores how love of neighbor also aids the pursuit of holiness—even in the midst of ordinary tasks like clearing some brush or serving a meal in Jesus' name. Whether we realize it or not, these tasks, performed in worship to God and in service to a neighbor, have transforming effects that conform us to Christ and make us holy. To see this more clearly, we need to see how our discussions of calling and community in chapter 4 relate to the development of the fruit of the Spirit in our lives.

DEVELOPING THE FRUIT OF THE SPIRIT

I often ask my students how they acquire the fruit of the Spirit. Does it simply appear in a person's life one day? Does God simply decide, "Today, I will make this person gentle, because she's asked me enough"?

The first response usually is, "Yes, God does simply decide. If you ask God in prayer, He will give you the fruit of the Spirit in the same way He might decide to heal you." This first response does not take into account the difference between God healing the physical body and God healing the whole person, body and soul. God can cure a physical disease in a moment in the same way that some medications can cure physical diseases, but God cannot make us holy in a moment, because to do so would violate the role we play in salvation through our free choice.

Paul tells us that we must keep in step with the Spirit, which implies that we must choose to cooperate with the Spirit's work in our lives. When we pray and ask God to help us become gentle, we are asking the Spirit to empower us to do gentle deeds among the community of faith and the larger community to which we belong. As James insists, faith without works is dead (2:14-26). Or, to put it in Paul's words, "the only thing that counts is faith *working* through love" (Galatians 5:6, emphasis mine). Only the faith that keeps in step with the Spirit by performing good works of love for our neighbor develops the fruit of gentleness, kindness, and so forth.

In chapter 5, I suggested that what we believe about predestination affects how we think God works in the world, especially His dealing with humans. If we think that God's predestination works in concert with free choice, then we should assume that God always works this way. God does not allow us the freedom to choose Christ initially and then prevent us from choosing otherwise. We always remain free to choose or not to choose Christ, which applies to keeping in step with the Spirit.

A second objection usually emerges at this point: "When I ask God to give me the fruit of the Spirit, how is that violating my free choice?" Once we see how we develop the fruit of the Spirit, the answer to this question will become clear. Let me begin by pointing out that when Paul lists various fruit of the Spirit, he is simply describing a list of virtues or character traits.[1] In fact, Paul provides these lists for his readers in several

Galatians 5:22, 23	**2 Corinthians 6:6**
love, joy, peace, patience, kindness, generosity, faithfulness, gentleness, self-control	*purity, patience, love, holiness of spirit, kindness, knowledge*
Colossians 3:12	**Philippians 4:8**
compassion, kindness humility, meekness, patience	*true, honorable, pure, pleasing, commendable, just*

Scripture passages (2 Corinthians 6:6; Galatians 5:22, 23; Philippians 4:8; Colossians 3:12).

As Gordon Fee notes, Paul calls these character traits "fruit of the Spirit" because he wants to highlight the fact that they grow in believers from the Spirit's work.[2] Consequently, it would be wrong to draw the conclusion that believers should remain passive and simply ask the Spirit to produce this fruit suddenly. Instead, Paul's admonition that his readers must walk with the Spirit (Galatians 5:25) implies that this fruit grows gradually as the believer cooperates with the work of the Spirit. This should convince us that we must choose to cooperate with the Spirit every step of the journey, but there are other reasons also.

What Paul describes as *fruit*, we normally call "character traits" or "virtues." Virtues or character traits are life skills. A skill is something that must be developed over time. While a person may have the natural talent to play baseball, he must develop the skills that go along with playing the game. He develops these skills gradually as he practices. The same point could be made about other activities like singing, carpentry, cooking, public speaking or playing an instrument.

Skills, like eye-hand coordination, help *perfect* or *complete* the baseball player, causing him to play the game well. Sandy Koufax pitched the perfect game because he had developed the skills that go hand in hand with pitching. Without those skills, Koufax would never have learned to control his fast ball and would never have been able to pitch the perfect game.

The important point about skills is that they complete or perfect the person by helping him develop his complete potential. Flourishing comes after the skills have been fully developed. Like any other set of skills, Paul's life skills only come through practice—the practice of living the Christian life as the Spirit empowers, guides and directs. No one becomes gentle without performing gentle actions over and over again in the same way that no one becomes a good baseball player without swinging a bat or throwing a baseball over and over again. God does not instantly make us gentle or kind, but He empowers us daily to perform gentle actions so that, over the course of our lives, we become gentle and kind. This is how God works in concert with our free choices to make us holy.

For Paul, an individual takes on the character of God by developing these life skills. Those who fully develop all of the fruit of the Spirit no longer need the Law because they possess the very character of Christ. The Law is written upon the heart of the person who fully possesses the fruit of the Spirit. In the same way that Sandy Koufax naturally did what the rules of pitching required because he had acquired the skills of pitching, so Christians naturally do what the law of God requires because they have the fruit.

Holiness and transformation are the equivalent of putting on the character of Christ. When we talk about someone having *character*, we usually mean that the person has a set of habits or ingrained dispositions. A *habit* refers to a pattern of behavior that results either from an addiction to some chemical or from repeating the same activity. The habit of smoking is a result of the addictive nature of nicotine. However, the habit of lying is a result of someone telling one lie after another until a pattern of behavior develops. If a person lies enough times, he predisposes himself to tell another lie. That is, he cultivates an ingrained disposition to lie. Once the person has a habit or an ingrained disposition, he has the character of a liar.

While I have described two bad habits, the same is true of good habits. When Paul calls gentleness a *fruit of the Spirit*, he means that gentleness is a habit or ingrained disposition that results from our working in cooperation with the Spirit. Once we have the habit in place, we can say that we have put on that characteristic of Christ. The goal of the Christian life is to put on the character of Christ by developing the habits that predispose us to act like Christ.

IMITATING CHRIST

Putting on the character of Christ involves a transformation from one set of character traits to another. We are attempting to cultivate a pattern of thought and behavior that reflects Christ's own life. Theologians have described this approach to holiness as an "imitation of Christ," because it suggests that we are striving to imitate Christ in all that we say and do.

One of the ways we seek to imitate Christ is by looking at His teachings and actions. What did Christ say about loving our neighbor? How did He treat people?

How did He show compassion? How did He display love? In what way did He humble Himself? Answering these questions requires a close examination of the Gospels. By examining the story of Jesus, we can begin to glimpse an alternative way of living in the world. Jesus teaches us how to live as members of an alternative reality, the kingdom of God. To put it in another way, Jesus is showing us a new kind of humanity where we relate to one another and to God in righteous ways. He is revealing what it means to be truly human. It is a new way of living that requires a new set of character traits.

In the Sermon on the Mount, Jesus indicated what it means to live in the world differently. Like Moses before Him, He was handing out the law of God. However, there is an important difference. Jesus was not simply receiving the Law from God and then communicating it to the people. Instead, He was giving the law of God. He was not simply a new Moses, He was more than Moses. Throughout the beginning of the Sermon, Jesus repeatedly said, "You have heard that it was said . . . but I say to you" (Matthew 5:21, 22, 27, 28, 31-34, 38, 39, 43, 44) to emphasize the fact that He was teaching a different kind of life than the law Moses taught. This new kind of life does not discard the law of Moses; instead, it moves beyond it. "Be perfect, just as your Father in heaven is perfect" (v. 48, *NKJV*).

Dietrich Bonhoeffer calls this command "extraordinary" because it points us to a life of undivided love in which we reflect God's love as exemplified in Christ's willingness to love to the uttermost by dying on a cross. When we read this passage, we can understand why Dietrich Bonhoeffer titles his examination of the Sermon on the Mount, *The Cost of Discipleship.* Christ is teaching a new way of living that is nothing less than the "extraordinary." [3]

A closer look at the Sermon helps us decipher how Jesus proposes that we go beyond the Law. Jesus is not as interested in external behavior as He is in internal behavior.[4] For example, He wants us to be poor in spirit (humble), mourners (those who compassionately weep with others in their tragedies), meek (gentle), peace-makers (just), merciful and so forth (5:1-12).

All of these traits relate to internal attitudes that we must develop. The person who possesses the qualities of meekness, mercy and peacemaking will also have the self-control not to lash out in anger and curse his brother or sister (see 5:21-26). Jesus is asking individuals to reshape their lives by a new set of character traits that are similar to Paul's list of the fruit of the Spirit. By these new character traits or habits, Jesus shows us how to fulfill the Law.

Let me now make a comment that may seem controversial at first. If all we do is examine the life and teachings of Christ in order to put on the character of Christ, we have not done enough. The problem is not that the teachings of Christ are deficient or irrelevant in any way; rather, it has to do with the distance between us and Christ. We live in the 21st century, while Christ lived in the 1st century. The difficulties we face are not always the same as those Christ faced. Sometimes we try to apply Christ's actions and teachings to a variety of situations Christ himself never faced. For example, Jesus did not deal with modern entertainment, owning and driving a car, investing, consumer credit, or in vitro fertilization. We can draw implications from Jesus' words and actions to deal with these issues, but we should recognize what we are doing.

Jesus was never in a situation where the choice was to lie and protect the Jews in your basement or tell the truth and give them up to the Nazis, knowing they would be murdered. He never asked the question of whether driving a Mercedes was too much. There was never a question about investing in a business with morally questionable practices or investing in an IRA that has shares in a company with questionable moral practices. He did not face the dilemma of whether a defense attorney should attack and impugn the testimony of an honest witness in the service of defending his client. As important as the teachings and life of Christ are, we should recognize that they simply do not cover every situation we will encounter as 21st-century Christians.

We must respond to this difficulty by becoming people of character. Our actions not only shape our character, they also come from it. If we walk in the Spirit, we will construct the character of Christ in us. The person with a kind disposition will have an easier time discerning what the kind response to a situation must be than the person who is prone to angry outbursts. The one who has angry outbursts will be more likely to engage in a rash action he will regret. His anger may blind him to the truth about the proper response.

The person who has a habit of truth-telling will have an easier time figuring out what it means to tell the truth in a particular situation than the person who has the habit of lying. The individual who practices the just treatment of other persons will be better situated to consider what the just action must be than the individual who constantly treats people unjustly. By keeping in step with the Spirit, slowly over the course of our lives we become people of character, which guides us in our actions and helps us to discover the truth as to what we should do.

A second difficulty arising from the distance between us and Christ can be easily seen in a story commonly told in sermons. The story is of a little child who was afraid of the dark and could not sleep. Initially, the father went into the child's room and reminded her that he and her mother were in the next room, so there was no need to be afraid. Of course, the child wasn't comforted, so the father said, "Jesus is here with you." The reply was, "I need Jesus with skin on Him."

The child's reaction implies that there is a great distance between Jesus and us. We cannot see or listen to Jesus anymore, and the child recognized this fact. In the New Testament, Jesus does not address every situation of His day, let alone ours. Christ is no longer present to show us how to handle situations. Jesus is not a *living* example to us that we can watch. When I say "living example," I don't mean to imply that Jesus is not alive. I'm simply asserting that He is no longer walking around on Planet Earth, teaching us and providing us an example of character. What is implicit in the child's comment is the need for a *living* Jesus who will serve as an example. We need a person or group of people who will model Christian behavior and with whom we can discuss all of the dilemmas we face. In short, we need the church.

A COMMUNITY OF CHARACTER

All of this talk about the need to cultivate the character of Christ in our lives leads us toward the community of disciples to which we must belong. The need for other people in our lives becomes apparent when we consider that we form our character as we develop a set of skills or habits.[5] The formation of character requires other people for at least three reasons. First, the old saying that "character is caught, not taught" suggests that we learn about good character from other people. Character can be caught only when others with good character are present. We also need other people with whom we can practice righteous acts. A kind action requires another human being who is the recipient of our kindness. Finally, we need people who will help us discover exactly where sin blinds us. We are all blind to the truth in some way and none of us can recognize all of the ways in which sin blinds us.

These three reasons tell us how important it is to belong to a community of believers. God calls believers to be part of His body because body life produces disciples. We learn how to put on Christ as we participate in body life. In the body of Christ we find good examples of righteous character, the opportunity to perform righteous deeds, and the insight into our own behavior.

Let me deal with the first and last points together. It is important to be surrounded by people of character who can serve as guides in our attempt to learn how to love our neighbors. As we watch how others act, we mimic their actions in our lives. In this way, character slowly forms in us because we gradually, sometimes imperceptibly, conform our lives to those around us.

I can recall moments in my childhood where I "caught" from my parents and others in my church what it means to be Christlike. I remember when my mother allowed my cousin to move in with us. As a teenager caught up in his own world, I wholeheartedly protested this decision. I did not like my cousin, and now I was being asked to live with her. I will never forget my mother's response: "Son, she needs our help. What do you want me to do? Turn her away?" In that brief moment, I saw compassion in action, and it knocked me out of my own selfishness. Although I did not realize it at the time, I had just "caught" some character from my mother.

There was another moment in the life of my church I will not forget. Our church was collectively deciding whether to split into two congregations. Most people were forced to choose a side. Families were divided.

One night, we were having a church-wide discussion

about the issue. The appropriate church officials were present to help the church decide if a split was absolutely necessary. During that meeting, one woman, who rarely voiced her opinion publicly, stood up and said that she was willing to leave rather than see the church split. As she spoke, I saw her courage and humility in action. Here was a woman who would give up her place in a church where she had been for 10 or more years if it would bring peace. She helped me "catch" the virtues of courage and humility.

While no one has perfect character, it is important to belong to a community of character—a community that reflects the kind of character we want to develop. This is not to say that we wait to belong to the church. When we become Christians, we become part of the church. As the body of Christ, the church is a community of disciples actively seeking to be led by the Spirit and to put on the character of Christ. This is the community to which we belong, which means that we must be part of a local church. By seeking to be a community of character, the church fosters an environment where Christians learn what it means to be Christian.

To become part of a community of disciples is to open up to their influence, as well as to exercise influence on them. This is the essence of accountability. The closer we get to other people, the more they know about us. Growing up in the U.S., I realize how uncomfortable this vulnerability is for us. We prefer the comfort of our privacy to the discomfort of learning to relate to others. Privacy is always more comfortable because one is rarely challenged to grow and change. However, to become all that we can be in Christ, we need to hear the voice of the Spirit speaking through our fellow believers. This is not about one group having authority over us; rather, it is about being open to the influence of others. When the church becomes a place where believers influence and are influenced by one another, it begins to be a place where healing and wholeness can occur.

Many Christians have a go-it-alone mentality. They believe that they can live their Christian lives by attending church on Sunday morning and not being invested in a community. What these Christians fail to realize is how blind they are to their own self-destructive behavior. In the midst of the give-and-take of community life, we learn about ourselves and our weaknesses.

God also uses us to teach others about themselves. When faced with a fellow Christian who gives until it hurts, the Spirit might challenge us to look at our own selfishness. As one man watches another treating his wife with care and concern, he might be led to see how neglectful he has been. Whenever we live a solitary Christian life, we become anemic Christians who fail to grow in grace.

Finally, the fruit of the Spirit must be practiced. The practice of kindness, gentleness, and other fruit, occurs in and through the community of disciples to which we belong. A second place where we practice the fruit of the Spirit is in the world where we live and minister.

While I have spent much of this chapter discussing

the role of the church in forming our character, this should not be taken as a lack of concern for loving our neighbors outside the church. The church cannot be God's community unless, like God, it remains open to the world. This means that our local churches must extend God's hand to outsiders and invite them to be part of the fellowship of faith. Practicing the fruit of the Spirit means forming Christ's character in all of our actions, within the community of faith and as an extension of the community of faith.

The Spirit is at work throughout the entire process of learning to love our neighbor. Sometimes, the Spirit prompts us to respond to another person with an act of kindness. At other times, the Spirit uses a fellow believer to challenge our views about some issue. The Spirit works in our lives within the context of the body and not apart from it. By responding to the Spirit's voice, we cooperate with God's effort to construct the character of Christ in us, and heal us of the self-destructive patterns of behavior that have dominated our lives.

THE POWER OF NEIGHBOR LOVE

The practice of neighbor love is a transforming activity that requires change. We must repent of sinful patterns of behavior and thought that prevent us from fully expressing neighbor love. In this respect, there is little difference between Paul's desire for us to develop the fruit of the Spirit and Christ's call to be His disciples. Both the fruit of the Spirit and the characteristics of Christ's disciples deal with the development of life skills or habits that reflect a new humanity. Christ wants us to take on His own righteous character, which exemplifies the character of God. For Paul, we put on the righteous character of Christ by walking in the Spirit over the course of our lives. As we practice neighbor love, we conform our lives to Christ.

Constructing Christ's character within us is about the gradual movement from one kind of life to another. We make this journey one choice at a time. By choosing to cooperate with the Spirit, we slowly develop righteous habits that bring about our transformation. This transforming journey is about God slowly healing us and enabling us to fulfill our complete potential as members of His new humanity. This movement from one kind of life to another is good for us because it enables us to be all that we were intended to be.

Another way of describing the transforming journey of neighbor love is "practicing the presence of God."[6] This means we view each action and choice as directed toward God. Even the choices to love our neighbor can and should be directed toward God. When we view our actions in this way, they are a form of worship.

As Paul admonishes us, we must present our bodies as living sacrifices, which is a spiritual act of worship (Romans 12:1). Becoming a living sacrifice involves pouring out one's life for others. This is what Christ did, and this is what neighbor love demands. Our worship to God occurs in the midst of everyday tasks when we give our service to others. How is this any different from James' claim that pure religion is visiting orphans and widows and keeping oneself unstained from the world (1:27)? Whether one identifies it as pure religion or true worship, it is seeing each choice to love a neighbor as a choice to love God.

Paul follows the admonition to present ourselves as living sacrifices with a command to be transformed by renewing our minds (12:2). We transform our patterns of thinking and behaving by engaging in the kind of behavior appropriate to a living sacrifice. When we choose to serve our neighbors, we change the way we think about them and ourselves. Giving a cup of water in Jesus' name helps us to become kind, because it involves a conscious choice to engage in an act of kindness. It also helps us to see the hurting and op-pressed through the eyes of God.

We are being made holy by these actions. That is, God is pouring out His own life into us as we choose to cooperate with the Spirit in performing acts of kindness, gentleness, and so forth. As we worship the Lord by serving our neighbor, we are united more closely with the Lord of Glory who did not consider equality with God something to be grasped (see Philippians 2:3-8). This new way of life that teaches us to be human also becomes the means by which we achieve wholeness.

The community of Christ's disciples to which we belong models a new way of living for us and becomes the place where we practice the presence of God. The church is the temple of the Spirit, because it is the place where the Spirit is fashioning new people who reflect the beauty of God in their lives.

We practice holiness as we seek to relate righteously to fellow believers. Likewise, we learn about holiness as we watch our fellow believers relate righteously to one another. Since every believer is still on the
journey toward perfection, we encourage holiness in
one another through forgiveness, consolation and,
sometimes, confrontation. In all these ways, the community seeks to model what behavior should be like in
the kingdom of God.

The church also has a mission to bring this new way
of living to the world. This means that acts of kindness
should not be reserved for fellow believers. Believers
do not separate from the world by sealing themselves
off from others. We separate ourselves from the world
by engaging in a form of behavior that challenges the
world to reflect the character of God. Instead of con-
tributing to the destructive patterns of behavior that
make up the world, believers should work against those
patterns of behavior by modeling Christ.

If Christ shows us what it means to be human, when
the church models Christ, the world will recognize
itself. The world will see in Christians not what it is, a
place where the slavery of sinful thinking and behaving dominate, but what it could be and should be. It
will recognize in Christians what it means to lift up
fellow human beings rather than beat them down—
what it means to love and be loved. In short, the world
will gain a glimpse of what it means to be human in
the community of Christ's disciples. This is how the
church continues God's mission in the world.

SUMMARY

The argument has now come full circle. Our worship to God is expressed both in terms of love for God and love for neighbor. In its fullest sense, worship is seeing God as the only One who can help us reach our complete potential. From the beginning, we were designed to be in relationship with God and to express that relationship by righteously relating to one another. True love for God *is* love for neighbor, and true love for neighbor *is* love for God. This is what holiness is and what holiness does.

Our pursuit of holiness is a quest to be transformed by the triune God of grace so that we can reflect this God in all that we say and do. In the end, there should be no separation between loving God and loving our neighbor, because both are part of the same fabric of healthy, whole and holy relations.

ENDNOTES

[1] See Dunn, *Theology of Paul*, 662-665; and Gordon Fee, *God's Empowering Presence*, 443-454.

[2] Fee, 443, 444.

[3] Dietrich Bonhoeffer, *Cost of Discipleship*, 171.

[4] See Ellen T. Charry, *By the Renewing of Your Minds: The Pastoral Function of Christian Doctrine* (New York: Oxford UP, 1997) 61-83.

[5] I have drawn some of the ideas for this section from Stanley Hauerwas' discussions of the church. See *The Peaceable Kingdom: A Primer in Christian Ethics* (Notre Dame: University of Notre Dame Press, 1983) 96ff; and *A Community of Character: Toward a Constructive Christian Social Ethic* (Notre Dame: University of Notre Dame Press, 1981) 111ff.

[6] See Brother Lawrence of the Resurrection, *The Practice of the Presence of God*, trans. with an intro. J.J. Delaney (New York: Doubleday, 1996).

CHAPTER 9

A View From the End

Then I saw a new heaven and a new earth; for the first heaven and the first earth had passed away, and the sea was no more. And I saw the holy city, new Jerusalem, coming down out of heaven from God, prepared as a bride adorned for her husband; and I heard a loud voice from the throne saying, "Behold, the dwelling of God is with men. He will dwell with them, and they shall be his people, and God himself will be with them; he will wipe away every tear from their eyes, and death shall be no more, neither shall there be mourning nor crying nor pain any more, for the former things have passed away" (Revelation 21:1-4, *RSV*).

A s a conclusion to this brief look at holiness, we will consider the nature of the end of all things. This could be summed up with one word: *shalom*. It is the condition in which peace and justice embrace in harmony. Isaiah captures shalom in the image of a lion lying down with a lamb to bring together God's purpose for humanity and the universe (see 11:6).

God's shalom involves His bringing into harmony all things under Himself, which happens through Christ in the Spirit. When humans attain the beauty of perfection, they find shalom—peace within themselves, peace with one another, peace with creation and peace with God. This is the ultimate purpose of holy living—to be made one with God and to be at peace.

When we arrive at shalom, we arrive at perfection. The kind of "perfection" I have in mind may be better described by the word *completion*. It is not an absolute perfection, because only God can be absolutely perfect. Instead, we become perfect in the sense that we have completely realized our potential as human beings so that we lacking nothing. To lack nothing does not imply that we no longer need God. Even in our perfected state, God must support us. Since, as humans, our very existence remains dependent on God, part of arriving at perfection in which we lack nothing involves entering into full, or complete, participation in God. To lack a relationship with God is to remain incomplete.

SHALOM

Shalom is what Cornelius Plantinga identifies as "the way things ought to be." Plantinga goes on to define *shalom* in this way:

> The webbing together of God, humans, and all creation in justice, fulfillment, and delight is what the Hebrew prophets call shalom. We call it peace, but it means far more than mere peace of mind or a cease-fire between enemies. In the Bible, shalom means universal flourishing, wholeness, and delight—a rich state of affairs in which natural needs are satisfied and natural gifts fruitfully employed, a state of affairs that inspires joyful wonder as its Creator and Savior opens doors and welcomes the creatures in whom he delights.[1]

The wholeness or flourishing that is shalom is the way the world was intended to be before sin entered the picture. A close reading of Genesis 1 reveals a world in balance and harmony. God created all things by bringing order to the chaos. After the opening verse, the writer states, "The earth was a formless void and darkness covered the face of the deep" (v. 2). The terms *formless* and *void* point to a hideous abyss or desert wasteland. Out of this shapeless and lifeless state, God begins to weave together a beautiful world where everything has its proper place.

It is no mistake that the writer uses the verb *separate* five times in the course of the opening chapter (vv. 4, 6, 7, 14, 18). When God creates, He brings symmetry and structure by separating things from one another. Every object in Creation has its role to play in the world—the light, the waters, the dry land, the vegetation, the animals—all take their rightful place. It is a world at peace, where everything flourishes through harmonious balance. It is shalom.

Shalom is what the Old Testament prophets longed for. When Jeremiah looks at the nation of Israel, he finds that her sinfulness has negated God's shalom. "I beheld the earth, and indeed it was without form, and void; and the heavens, they had no light" (Jeremiah 4:23, *NKJV*). What Jeremiah sees is literally "uncreation," a reversal of God's creative work.

Sin disintegrates the wholeness of God's Creation. The disease of sin produces a world that constantly vandalizes God's shalom.[2] It is the cascading effect of no longer living in fellowship with God. When Jeremiah looks at Israel, he laments the fact that the chaos and disorder out of which God made the world has now returned. Through Jeremiah, we see how sin pollutes the entire created order by breaking down relationships in fundamental ways. There is no peace, only confusion and disorder, fighting and disintegration.

Into this state, Isaiah announced, "Unto us a Child is born . . . and His name will be called Wonderful, Counselor, Mighty God, Everlasting Father," and finally, "Prince of Peace"(9:6, *NKJV*). This heir to David's throne will usher in God's reign of shalom once again.

Drawing on the establishment of shalom, Paul makes it clear that Christ is "our peace," because in His life and death, He is restoring a wholeness of relations among people (Ephesians 2:14-18). Where there is division and strife resulting from vandalism of God's shalom, Christ is preaching peace to those far off and those near with the express aim of creating a new humanity. Although Christ has won this peace through His death on the cross, it must be actualized in the world. Paul sees this occurring by means of the Spirit, who opens up the way to the Father (v. 18). The full realization of God's shalom will come as the Spirit unites all persons in Christ to the glory of the Father.

When we turn to the Book of Revelation, we discover that the story ends with the restoration of God's shalom through the triumphant Lamb. As the seventh angel announces after he blows his trumpet, "The kingdoms of this world have become the kingdoms of our Lord and of His Christ" (Revelation 11:15, *NKJV*). The image of Jesus as the Lamb slain points toward the death of Christ. The One who has conquered is none other than the One who suffered and died (see 5:6).

John, like Paul, suggests that the victory has yet to be realized fully. The Lamb who was slain must return on a white horse to establish God's righteous reign of peace once and for all. John sees Christ, the spotless Lamb, returning on a white horse as the heavens open (19:11). The robe of Christ, dipped in blood, suggests a reference to His death, even as He comes in power and glory. He is described as "Faithful and True," because He is the Word of God who was faithful and is the Truth. As Richard Bauckham notes, Christ is coming as the Truth to dispel the lies of the Beast.[3] All of the deception and blindness brought on by sin will be removed one day as Christ comes in His glory.

Revelation concludes with a vivid contrast between two ways of living, the New Jerusalem and Babylon.[4] For John, the city of Babylon symbolized Rome in its economic might (17—18). Because of economic prosperity, Rome was as attractive and deceptive as any harlot. It dominated the world and sought to seduce all people through its wealth and splendor.

During John's day, Rome heralded itself as the empire that brought peace. One of the slogans of the time was *Pax Romana* (Roman Peace). To John, this slogan was no more than a piece of propaganda, advertising a way of life that really brought destruction and death.[5] In the end, Babylon is a symbol for the destructive nature of life outside of God. As the opposite of God's shalom, Babylon exemplifies the fruit of the disease of sin, which John describes as the plagues of death, mourning and famine (18:8).

The New Jerusalem is the divine alternative to Babylon. It is portrayed as a place, a people and a presence.[6] When John sees it coming down from heaven, he first describes it as a bride (21:1, 2). This description is immediately followed with an announcement that the dwelling, or tabernacle, of God will now be with humanity (v. 3). In these three verses, John depicts the New Jerusalem as a people (the bride) and as the presence of God. No temple exists in this new city because God's presence will permeate every part of it.

In addition, there is no crying, weeping, pain or death. Instead, God's own life will flow out from His throne and enliven all things (22:1). Like a divine environmental cleanup program, God's presence will immediately remove all the spiritual pollution and hazardous waste left over from the world's sinful state. Finally, God's presence will produce a new paradise, or new creation. It is the New Jerusalem (shalom), the city of peace—God's final peace.

John's description of the New Jerusalem will possess unsurpassed beauty. This beauty is to be a reflection of the glory of God. Richard Bauckham points out the connection between John's description of God as being like jasper (4:3) and the New Jerusalem as having a light like a jasper jewel (21:11). Bauckham states, "John probably means that the whole city . . . shines with the reflected glory of God himself."[7]

Like the Tabernacle and the Temple, the New Jerusalem is set apart unto God by its splendor and radiance. The shalom that characterizes it will give rise to this

beauty. It is the beauty of God's own perfection reflected in the holiness of the bride, as well as the architec-
ture of the city itself. As the place of God's presence,
the New Jerusalem shows us how shalom and perfection go hand in hand. God's perfection gives rise to
beauty, harmony and order. It is the beauty of God's
own life, extended to His Creation. When we finally
arrive at the New Jerusalem—when we finally become
the New Jerusalem—we will reach our complete potential in the beauty of His holiness.

SOME BLESSINGS TO KEEP BEFORE US

Many blessings result from living a holy life. These
blessings are not primarily associated with material
possessions or the accumulation of worldly things—
the things affiliated with a way of life contrary to the
Christian vision. These are not to be identified with
the allure of Babylon. Rather, the blessings of holiness are bound up with its ultimate purpose: God
himself. We often mistakenly perceive these blessings as the end and seek after them, rather than their
Author. This mistaken perception relates to the first
commandment: "You shall have no other gods before
me." Perceiving God as merely the means to some
greater blessing violates that commandment. God
must always be the end—the ultimate point of all we
do—and never the means.

If God is the end and the blessings of holiness are
bound up with that end, then an individual receives
those blessings in proportion to sharing God's own life.

To put it simply, the more we participate in God, the closer to God we become and the more we share His life. The aim of holiness is participation in the divine life of God. Its reward is sharing God's character and all it involves. The question is, what does it mean to participate in God as the final purpose of a holy life? The answer offered in this book is that holiness is about flourishing—achieving our complete potential as believers. We cannot achieve this potential on our own, nor were we designed to do so. God created us in His image, which suggests that God made us to achieve our potential as we participate in His life. What are the blessings of sharing God's own life?

1. *The first blessing of participation is stability.* Instability characterizes human existence. We are buffeted by the winds of change constantly. Events and circumstances remain out of our control. We experience sickness and death. We spend a lifetime getting to know people, developing friends, loving our spouse and pouring our lives into our children, only to have the people we love slowly ripped away from us. We crave stability, even while we experience nothing but instability.

When my uncle died, I remember becoming aware of how unstable my life was. As I was preparing for my 10-minute eulogy, it suddenly dawned on me that the people in my life whom I had come to count on were beginning to slip away. As a child, I viewed my uncle and others as stable forces in my life. With my uncle's death, I realized that these people were leaving me. In one moment, I caught a glimpse of my future.

One day, everything I held dear in this world would be gone. All my friends and my family would finally be taken and I would be left with nothing. As if that were not enough to endure, one day I will breathe my last breath and say good-bye to this world. No matter how much I scratch and claw at life, I cannot even hang on to my own existence. Like everything else, it will leave me. When I think in this way, I glimpse what the writer of Ecclesiastes meant by "Vanity of vanities, all is vanity" (1:2, *NKJV*). Everything we do seems to be meaningless in light of the instability we face.

We cannot begin to understand what God is giving us unless we look death square in the face and see it for what it is: the final enemy. Death is the ultimate end of instability. It is the loss of all things. There is a kind of terror associated with death because we know deep down what it means. Although we spend a lifetime building a home and making our way in the world, it will all be stripped away. This is true for the rich and the poor, the president and the panhandler. All the instability death brings can create intense fear, leading to paranoia. We try desperately to hang on to the life we have made. However, all of our cautious behavior, watching the kids closely and being careful when we drive, will be in vain. Death is the final enemy that strips us of our dignity by ripping life out from under us.

Another dimension to our instability is the nature of our character. We want to be stable, making the right choices and being dependable, but our inconsistency

becomes evident every time we fail others and ourselves by making self-destructive choices. Whenever
we say to ourselves, "Why did I do that"? we are
acknowledging how unstable our character is. Although
some are more consistent than others, at some point we
all experience the instability of our character because no
one makes the right choices all the time.

In the face of our final enemy, we must remember
that the life of God is slowly renewing us. "Even though
our outer nature is wasting away, our inner nature is
being renewed day by day" (2 Corinthians 4:16). One
day we will be clothed with God's own stability. The
immortality and incorruption of God's own life will be
given to us. How do we know this? The same Spirit of
life who raised Jesus from the dead is our guarantee that
the life of God is pouring forth into our lives.

Christians need not fear the instability of life because
we know that we will put on immortality. This does not
mean that death, pain and dying are unreal, but it does
mean that they are defeated. In addition, Christians
should recognize that God is slowly giving us the stability of an incorruptible life. One day we will no longer
sin or make self-destructive choices; we will be like
God who always does the right thing.

2. *The second blessing of participation is beauty.*
Complete perfection entails perfect beauty. The beauty of perfection is absolute poetry in motion where
everything is in harmony, order and at rest. Some people may think that, at the end of all things, believers
will simply cease from activity, as though the beauty

of perfection will end in the heavenly equivalent of a day at the beach where the believer is simply sitting and soaking up the divine rays of love. This is how they interpret the teaching of Hebrews that a final rest awaits the people of God (4:1-11).

Such a view could not be further from the truth. As Harold Attridge suggests, the teaching of Hebrews remains contingent upon the idea of Sabbath rest.[8] Sabbath is not a time of inactivity—it involves celebration and praise. At the very least, this suggests that entering into God's rest will mean a continuous state of activity. The beauty of perfection is activity and rest at the same time.

To explain what I mean, let me return to Hebrews for a moment. In 4:3, the writer declares that "we who have believed *enter* that rest . . ." (emphasis mine). The verb *enter* is in the present tense, suggesting that believers are now participating in the rest of God. God's divine rest is not merely a future reality, but must be experienced in some way now.[9]

To make certain that his readers don't misunderstand him, the writer of Hebrews almost immediately says, "Let us . . . make every effort to enter that rest" (v. 11). We are entering the future rest now, but the full entrance into that rest will occur at some point in the future. This ought to tell us that Hebrews is not describing a place of complete rest, like the Promised Land was for the Israelites. Instead, the idea of rest is connected to salvation in Hebrews. Believers have entered salvation, but they have not completed it yet.

A complete understanding of rest depends on the way Hebrews understands salvation. Believers enter their rest fully when they are fully saved. For Hebrews, this means entering fully into God's presence. As we saw earlier, Jesus opens the way into God's presence through His own death on the cross. In fact, Hebrews calls Christ the "pioneer" or "captain" of our salvation (2:10; 6:20; 12:2), which suggests that Jesus is the model who both opens the way to God's presence and shows us how to enter that presence. The writer leaves little doubt as to how Jesus enters the presence of God. He is perfected by suffering (2:10) or learns obedience through suffering so that He is brought to perfection (5:7-10). As a result, the writer declares that God has a Son "who has been made perfect forever" (7:28).[10]

During His earthly ministry, Jesus labored at doing the will of God and experienced the sufferings and toils of this labor. It was this process that brought Jesus to completion, or perfection. As the model for believers, Jesus shows us that our laboring now involves a process of transformation that will lead to our perfection then as we enter fully into God's presence and experience God's own life. The fact that our consciences have been cleansed tells us that we have already entered God's presence, even if we must labor to enter completely.

Entering the presence of God is a process of transformation that requires growth in holiness. Believers must work and labor in the same way Jesus worked and labored. Our present work and labor involves toil and sweat. Earthly labor is a tiring and taxing activity, even if the activity itself is ultimately beneficial. Any person who has endured the long, hard hours of learning to play an instrument or play a sport knows that these labor-intensive times are difficult. Yet, the long hours of practice transform the person from someone who cannot play to someone who can. When the person finally develops all the skill necessary to play well, that person has completed the learning process.

Once the learning process is complete, the person does not cease from activity—he or she enters a new phase of activity. When Jesus enters into the presence of God, the writer of Hebrews does not describe Him ceasing from all activity. He stands at the right hand of the Father as a faithful High Priest who lives to make intercession for the saints (7:24, 25; 12:2).

How is this activity restful? It no longer involves the labor and toil of arriving at perfection. Instead, this activity is the fruit of a perfected life. The beauty of perfection is complete motion and stillness, activity and rest. Consider for a moment a musician who is at the peak of his or her craft. Although engaged in activity, the activity seems effortless because the musician is now experiencing the benefit of prior work.

When Sandy Koufax was pitching the perfect game, he was engaged in constant activity, but it was not tiresome. After the game, Koufax said that he could sense his arm getting stronger as he pitched. Even with these earthly activities, we can see that there comes a point where we move beyond labor and toil to the experience of rest right in the midst of our activity. Like the hummingbird beats its wings in a rapid motion and yet remains still, we enter a new phase in which we remain active and experience rest.

When we fully participate in the beauty of God's perfection, we will know what it means to work without labor—to be active and rested at the same time. The beauty of perfection is reflecting divine poetry in motion in which everything works so harmoniously that we simply relax and enjoy.

If you have ever been engaged in an activity and suddenly stopped thinking about what you were doing and simply enjoyed the activity itself, then you have an idea of what life will be like when we enter God's presence. There are no worries about making mistakes, no pressure to sustain concentration. Instead, what we do will be so natural to us that it will seem like we're not doing anything at all. This is the blessing of participating in beauty of God's perfection.

3. *The third blessing of participation is love.* This is the happy ending. The beloved gets her Lover—the bride finally possesses her Bridegroom and gains all she could ever desire. The consummation of holiness finds its ultimate expression in the embrace of two lovers who have been separated for too long. As Biblical exegetes from the Middle Ages knew well, the Song of Songs sums up the Christian life: a full embrace of her lover by the Beloved. Christians must be careful not to become sidetracked by too literal a perception of what this means. Modern society has so shaped our understanding of sexual relations that sometimes we fail to

understand what is involved in such an encounter. Human beings are sexual, not simply to engage in a physical exchange, but to enter into an intimate activity of giving and receiving, which is reflective of the inner life of God as a communion of love.

God exists as a communion of love. The Father, the Son and the Holy Spirit all give and receive love from one another. Theologians have described this give-and-take of love as the "divine dance." When God invites us to share His life, He is inviting us to enter the dance of love between Father, Son and Holy Spirit. This is ultimately what it means to be the bride of Christ.

Remember, the bride is not one believer, but the host of the redeemed who are joined in union with Father, Son and Holy Spirit. Consequently, the dance I am describing is not a dance between each believer and God, but between all believers and God. All believers are caught up in that divine embrace in which the Father, the Son and the Holy Spirit take their hands and usher them into the joy of God's own life. To dance is to be taken up—raptured as it were—in the all-encompassing, overwhelming, indescribable joy of the presence of the triune Godhead, who unifies all things in Christ Jesus! As C.S. Lewis states:

> It is only in our "hours off," only in our moments of permitted festivity, that we find an analogy [for the end]. Dance and game are frivolous, unimportant down here; for "down here" is not their natural place. Here, they are a moment's rest from the life we were placed here to live. But in this world everything is upside down. That which, if it could be prolonged

here, would be a truancy, is likest that which in a better country is the End of Ends. Joy is the serious business of heaven.[11]

4. *The final blessing of participation is happiness.* I hope by now that you can see how happiness and joy will arise naturally from the beauty of perfection and participating in the divine dance. Augustine says that only God is to be enjoyed properly speaking. To draw nearer to God is to enjoy divine bliss in ever-increasing measures. This bliss is described in Scripture as "joy inexpressible and full of glory" (1 Peter 1:8, *NKJV*).

Paul completely exhausts his supply of superlatives trying to express the inexpressible. By focusing on the rules of a holy life, we can sometimes forget its true purpose. God does not provide rules for the sake of rules. How morbid! Holiness is not about how well we perform, but how we are able to move onward and upward toward perfect happiness. Our goal should be the complete and utter joy that comes from experiencing the divine dance of Father, Son and Holy Spirit. It is a joy that arises naturally from our own activity, when we enter into a place of rest from the weariness of our labors and experience the joy of doing something. If the goal is the complete joy that comes from God himself, it is easy to understand why Paul would declare that he presses on toward the mark of the high calling in Christ.

FOR OUR SAKES HE BECAME POOR

In drawing our discussion to a close, we need to listen once again to the angels' song of the sweet silent night, the holy night into which the eternal Word of God first entered our life that He might invite us to enter His. The song that the angels sing is a new song. It is God's concerto in which the first verse begins, "Glory to God in the highest, and on earth peace, good-will toward men" (Luke 2:14, *NKJV*) and the last verse concludes, "To the one seated on the throne and to the Lamb be blessing and honor and glory and might for-ever and ever" (Revelation 5:13).

In the first verse, we see the announcement that God is taking our poverty upon Himself. As Paul declares, "For your sakes he became poor" (2 Corinthians 8:9). This is the movement of Divinity toward humanity. When God became a human being, He willingly bank-rupted Himself, not only entering into the fragility of human existence, but also going to the margins of that existence, the forgotten and forsaken side of life. For the God of life intends to bring life to the deepest dark-est places of the world.

In the final verse of the song, we see all of Creation joining to bless the God who has blessed them and made them partakers of His life. This is the movement of humanity toward Divinity. When God became a man, He led humanity on a new exodus out of sin, death and judgment, not simply to a new life, but to His life—a life of holiness and happiness.

Try to imagine arriving at a place where we no longer sabotage ourselves by our words and deeds. The person-ality traits that conspire against us are gone. Some per-sons tend to become angry over little things and then do or say something regrettable. Others fight insecurities about themselves, which cause them not to risk and say something or do something they know they should. Still others may wrongly experience guilt for doing something they know is the right thing to do. Perfectionism may plague others, prompting them to question everything they do as never being good enough. Like a ball and chain wrapped around the neck, these traits are always present. But God invites us to begin a journey that will culminate in our complete liberation from these self-destructive tendencies. He beckons us to come with Him and enter the path of holiness.

The eternal Son became poor that we might become rich. The incarnate God experienced His first human breath that we might breathe the air of heaven. He covered Himself in the impoverished and abandoned scent of an unclean stable that we might be bathed in the aroma of His majesty and glory. He clothed Himself in the frailty of human flesh that we might put on the garment of His power and might. He has taken human flesh to lead humanity to its true home. This home is not simply a place. We would miss the true significance of salvation if we were to see it simply as acquiring a mansion on some hillside. Heaven is heaven because of God. It is the reflection of God's own beauty. We will also reflect the beauty of His perfection as we join the dance around the throne.

ENDNOTES

[1] Cornelius Plantinga, *Not the Way It's Supposed to Be* (Grand Rapids: Eerdmans, 1995) 10.

[2] Plantinga, 7ff.

[3] Richard Bauckham, *The Theology of the Book of Revelation* (Cambridge: Cambridge UP, 1993) 104-106.

[4] Bauckham, 126ff. See also Bauckham, *The Climax of Prophecy: Studies on the Book of Revelation* (Edinburgh: T & T Clark, 1993) 338ff; and R. Hollis Gause, *Revelation: God's Stamp of Sovereignty on History* (Cleveland, TN: Pathway, 1983) 219ff.

[5] Bauckham, *Climax of Prophecy*, 347.

[6] Bauckham, *Theology of Revelation*, 132ff.

[7] Bauckham, *Theology of Revelation*, 134.

[8] See Harold Attridge, *Hebrews*, 130, 131.

[9] Attridge, 126. See also David A. DeSilva, *Perseverance in Gratitude: A Socio-Rhetorical Commentary on the Epistle "to the Hebrews"* (Grand Rapids: Eerdmans, 2000) 155, 156.

[10] See Attridge, 197-199 and D. Peterson, *Hebrews and Perfection*, 74-103.

[11] C.S. Lewis, *The Joyful Christian: 127 Readings from C.S. Lewis* (New York: Macmillan, 1977) 228.